10/06

31.93

Attack of the Superbugs
The Crisis of Drug-Resistant Diseases

ISSUES IN FOCUS TODAY

Kathiann M. Kowalski

Enslow Publishers, Inc.

40 Industrial Road PO Box 38
Box 398 Aldershot
Berkeley Heights, NJ 07922 Hants GU12 6BP
USA UK

http://www.enslow.com

Library of Congress Cataloging-in-Publication Data

Kowalski, Kathiann M., 1955-
    Attack of the superbugs : the crisis of drug-resistant diseases / Kathiann M. Kowalski.
        p. cm. — (Issues in focus today)
    Includes bibliographical references and index.
    ISBN 0-7660-2400-8
    1. Drug resistance in microorganisms—Juvenile literature. I. Title. II. Series.
    QR177.K69 2005
    616.9'041—dc22

                                                    2005007067

Printed in the United States of America

10 9 8 7 6 5 4 3 2 1

To Our Readers:
We have done our best to make sure all Internet Addresses in this book were active and appropriate when we went to press. However, the author and the publisher have no control over and assume no liability for the material available on those Internet sites or on other Web sites they may link to. Any comments or suggestions can be sent by e-mail to comments@enslow.com or to the address on the back cover.

Illustration Credits: U.S. Centers for Disease Control and Prevention (CDC), pp. 51, 71, 81, 111, 119; CDC/Dr. Richard Facklam, pp. 8, 101; CDC/Jim Gathany, pp. 3, 69; CDC/A. Harrison, P. Feorino, and E.L. Palmer, pp. 12, 105; CDC/Dr. Holdeman, pp. 3, 34; CDC/Donald Kapanoff, pp. 63, 115; CDC/Joe Miller, p. 91; Evergreen State College, p. 86; Kathiann M. Kowalski, pp. 3, 29, 45, 48, 54, 84, 88, 96, 107, 109, photos courtesy of Pfizer, Inc., pp. 3, 5, 22, 24, 58, 61, 66, 73, 77, 103, 113, 117; Rubberball Productions, p. 42; photo courtesy of Anne Marie Seeholzer, pp. 1, 38; photo courtesy of Wyeth Pharmaceuticals, pp. 3, 15.

Cover Illustrations: U.S. Centers for Disease Control and Prevention/Dr. Richard Facklam (background); Photos.com (large illustration); BananaStock (small illustration).

C o n t e n t s

	Acknowledgments	4
Chapter 1	Superbugs Attack	5
Chapter 2	Battle Against the "Bugs"	15
Chapter 3	Prescription for Trouble?	29
Chapter 4	Not Just What the Doctor Ordered	42
Chapter 5	Special Problems	58
Chapter 6	Seeking Solutions	73
Chapter 7	Time for Decisions	88
	Chronology	98
	Chapter Notes	100
	Glossary	121
	For More Information	123
	Further Reading and Internet Addresses	124
	Index	125

Acknowledgments

The author gratefully thanks the following people for their help and assistance: Richard Besser, Centers for Disease Control and Prevention; George Fischler, The Dial Corporation; Elizabeth Kutter and Gautam Dutta, Evergreen State College; Jennifer Crandall and Stephen Lederer, Pfizer, Inc.; Stuart B. Levy, Tufts University and Alliance for the Prudent Use of Antibiotics; Eric and Alexandra McGinness and Anne Marie Seeholzer; Bethany Lynn Meissner; Janice Mitchell; John H. Powers, Food and Drug Administration; Steven Projan and Gerald Burr, Wyeth Pharmaceuticals.

This book is dedicated to my daughter, Bethany Meissner.

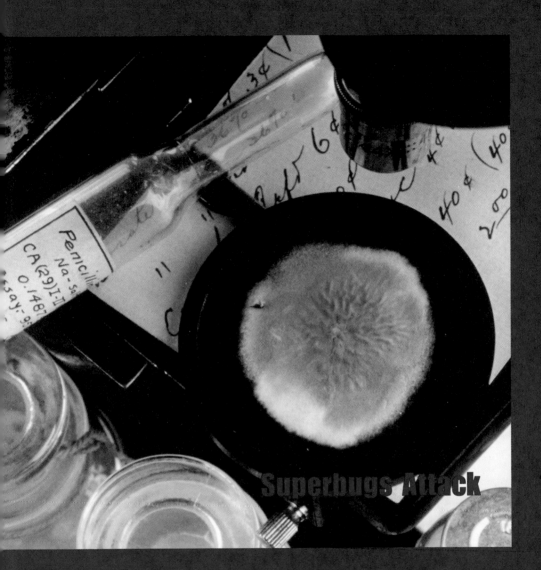

Brandon Hancock was looking forward to his second year at the University of Southern California (USC). He had finished his freshman year on the dean's list. Now he was set to become the Trojans' starting fullback. Then, at the last preseason practice, Brandon sprained his ankle and scraped his knee.

Practically overnight, Brandon's right knee swelled up. Ugly pus oozed out. The hospital admitted Brandon for a staph infection.

Staph is short for *Staphylococcus*. That group of bacteria lurks in soil and on many surfaces. *Staphylococcus aureus* is a type of staph that causes disease.

Usually, the body's skin and immune system prevent

infection. But sometimes staph eludes the body's defenses. The bacteria cause skin infections and fevers. In severe cases, deadly blood poisoning or bone infection can result.

Staph bacteria are microscopic. Yet these tiny organisms brought down the six-foot, one-inch, 235-pound football player. Brandon's fever raged over 100° F.

Doctors usually treat staph with antibiotics—drugs that kill bacteria or hinder its growth. Usually, penicillin or erythromycin does the job. If they do not, doctors can use methicillin. None of those medicines helped Brandon. He had a drug-resistant disease.

Brandon had methicillin-resistant *Staphylococcus aureus*, or MRSA. To fight it, doctors use powerful "last-resort" antibiotics, such as vancomycin. Often such medicines cost more and have stronger side effects. In rare cases, MRSA might resist those drugs too.

Brandon finally recovered. After several weeks, he started training again while his ankle sprain healed.

Brandon was lucky. He missed five games in the 2003 season, but he still got to play for the champion USC Trojans. Still, his case was puzzling. How did a healthy college student in peak condition get such a dangerous disease?[1]

Selective Pressure

How can diseases fight back against antibiotics? They lack any brains to plot or scheme. However, disease-causing microbes can reproduce quickly. Some bacteria reproduce every ten or twenty minutes. As generations pass, microbes evolve.

In the process of evolution, organisms with useful adaptations—traits that help them survive in their environment—are more likely to reproduce. Thus, they pass on those traits to their offspring. Charles Darwin called this trend "survival of the fittest."

In nature, microbes compete for space and food. To protect

their "turf," some organisms make natural antibiotics. The chemicals fight off other microbes. Thus, people did not invent antibiotics. They discovered them.

Likewise, people did not invent resistance to medicines. In nature, a few bacteria might survive attacks by natural antibiotics from other microbes. Such bacteria gain a competitive advantage—at least for a while.

Eventually, the competing species evolves to produce stronger natural antibiotics. In effect, an "arms race" is always going on between and among microbes. Their adaptations affect not just their own evolution, but also those of competing species. The net result is a rough balance of power.

Humans' use of antibiotics changed that. Suddenly, drug companies were making millions of pounds of antibiotics. The drugs kill all or most of the targeted bacteria. By chance, though, a few bacteria might not be susceptible to the drugs. By surviving, those bacteria are more likely to pass on resistance to bacteria in the future.

This process is known as *selective pressure*. Antibiotics kill most strains (types or varieties) of a bacterium. Ironically, though, that *selects*, or gives an advantage to, resistant strains. Those strains can then reproduce.

Crisis in the Community?

Brandon Hancock's bout with MRSA was not an isolated case. MRSA also struck six of his teammates. Three of them had to go to the hospital.

MRSA also struck a seventeen-year-old high school football player in Franklin, Wisconsin, in October 2003.[2] Earlier that year, two high school wrestlers in Indiana had MRSA.[3] And in late 2002, fifty students in Pasadena, Texas, had MRSA, including some football players.[4]

Infection can spread quickly in gyms and locker rooms.

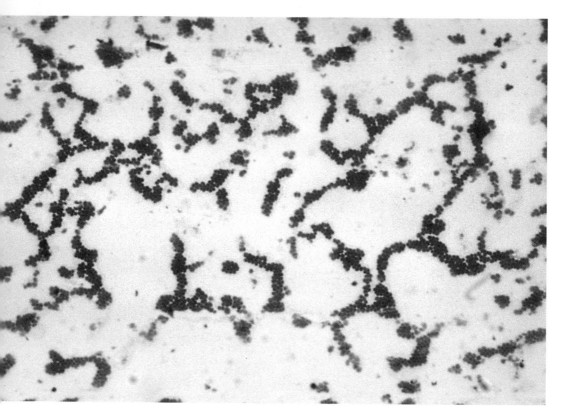

Staphylococcus aureus **is shown here, magnified 320 times. Brandon Hancock was infected with a resistant form of staph.**

Sometimes athletes share water bottles or towels. Often they use the same weight benches, whirlpool baths, and showers.

Other equipment can transmit germs too. When several members of a Colorado fencing club acquired MRSA, health officials suspected shared equipment was a possible culprit. Also, team members wore sensor wires under their clothes, and these wires had no set cleaning schedule.[5]

Athletes are not the only ones at risk for MRSA. A toddler in rural North Dakota got MRSA soon after she took antibiotics for an ear infection. The sixteen-month-old girl went into shock as her fever raged over 105° F. She died from respiratory failure and cardiac arrest.[6]

During the last decade, doctors have also encountered several drug-resistant staph infections that could resist even vancomycin.[7] Staph is not the only disease showing drug resistance, either. Respiratory and ear infections are becoming harder to treat. Foodborne infections now show resistance too. Sexually transmitted diseases, such as gonorrhea, are also a problem.

Compared to hospitals and other institutions, there are far fewer cases of drug-resistant diseases in the community. Yet the problem of "superbugs" is growing. Diseases that used to be cured easily are becoming harder to treat. Plus, it seems as if drug-resistant microbes can strike anywhere.

Institutional Risks

People go to the hospital to get well. But each year about 2 million people also get sick at American hospitals—often with drug-resistant diseases.[8] Hospital-acquired, or *nosocomial*, infections are nothing new.

Hospitals are in the business of healing people, so why do many people get sicker there? For one thing, disease or injury makes it harder for people to fight off infection. Some medications suppress the immune system too. Either way, sick patients are easy prey for infections.

A few bacteria are resistant—not susceptible—to particular antibiotics. They survive and pass on their resistance to the next generation of bacteria.

Very young patients may not be sick, but they often do not have well-developed immune systems either. In late 2003, several newborn boys got MRSA at a Long Island, New York, hospital.[9]

Hospital patients are often in close quarters too. Air circulating throughout a facility can spread germs. Sloppy hygiene can spread disease too. All these factors make it easier for diseases to infect patients. Thus, even patients who are generally healthy can get hospital infections. New mothers whose children were born without complications would be one example.

Hospitals' heavy antibiotic use is another factor that drives drug-resistant diseases. Patients get antibiotics when they have infections. Doctors prescribe antibiotics to prevent infections during and after surgery too.

The antibiotics help many people, but they also apply selective pressure. They wipe out most susceptible strains. That lets resistant bacteria thrive.

Over 70 percent of all hospital staph infections resist penicillin. About half resist methicillin as well.[10]

Health care institutions face a range of other superbugs too. *Streptococcus pneumoniae* can cause pneumonia, meningitis, and blood poisoning. *Pseudomonas aeruginosa* and *Klebsiella pneumoniae* cause dangerous lung diseases. *Enterococcus* bacteria can infect the blood, heart, and urinary tract.

Overall, about 10 percent of patients get nosocomial infections.[11] In the United States, that amounts to about 2 million people per year.[12] Nosocomial infections play a role in up to one hundred thousand deaths per year in the United States. A majority of those infections resist one or more commonly used antibiotics.[13] Battling such infections is an ongoing challenge.

Problems in Prisons

Infections spread quickly in prisons. Inmates live in close contact with each other. Hygiene is sometimes shoddy. Plus, doctors may not always spot drug-resistant diseases.

Nineteen-year-old Sean Schwamberger was serving an eleven-month sentence for forgery at an Ohio prison. He eventually hoped to become a house painter, but he never got the chance.

When Sean got a skin infection, the prison's medical staff diagnosed it as staph and gave him penicillin. But Sean had

MRSA, so the medicine did not work. With nothing to fight it off, his infection became worse. Eventually, Sean collapsed in the prison's recreation yard. Nine days later, the teenager died.[14]

The Ohio jail is not unique. In 2002, over nine hundred people at the Los Angeles County Jail had MRSA too. Over sixty of them went to the hospital. Ten had serious complications when the bacteria spread through their bodies.[15]

From Victory to Global Crisis

For over sixty years, antibiotics have worked medical miracles. They routinely cure diseases that used to be fatal. Often patients feel better after the first few doses. Plus, many antibiotics have few side effects.

Meanwhile, medical researchers have developed vaccines for polio, smallpox, and other dreaded viruses. With widespread vaccination programs, rates of infectious disease dropped drastically.

By the late 1960s, medical experts were declaring victory. "The time has come to close the book on infectious diseases," Surgeon General William Stewart said. "We have basically wiped out infection in the United States."[16]

Sadly, he spoke too soon. Since then, scientists have discovered more diseases. HIV, or human immunodeficiency virus, causes AIDS—acquired immunodeficiency syndrome. Since doctors first recognized it in 1981, the virus has infected over 40 million people worldwide.

Other newly discovered diseases affect fewer people. Yet they can still kill. Lyme disease, Hantavirus pulmonary syndrome, Ebola, and Marburg are just a few "emerging infectious diseases" that have struck in recent decades. West Nile virus has been around in Africa for a long time. Cases began showing up in the United States and Canada only within the last decade.

Other diseases are "re-emerging." Tuberculosis (TB) rates plunged after the discovery of antibiotics helped cure the lung

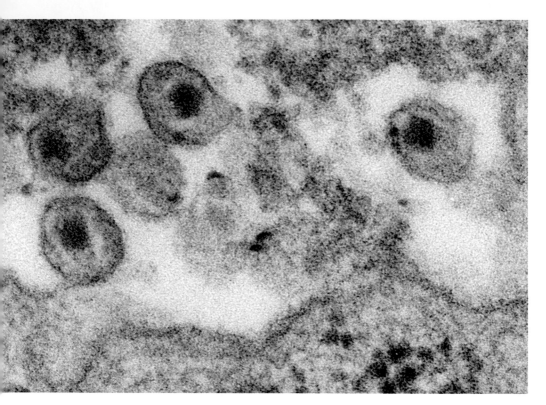

HIV, the virus that causes AIDS. Since its discovery in 1981, the virus has infected more than 40 million people.

disease. Yet rates are creeping back up. Now even the most powerful medicines cannot always cure TB.

Yesterday's wonder drugs are no longer "magic bullets" that can cure almost anything. "Diseases that seemed to be subdued, such as tuberculosis and malaria, are fighting back with renewed ferocity," announced the World Health Organization (WHO) in 1996. In the agency's view, problems with drug-resistant diseases, emerging diseases, cancer, and other issues added up to a "global crisis" in public health.[17] A decade later, that public health crisis still exists.

Drug-resistant diseases cause pain and anguish for individuals. They also carry huge costs to society. Total health care costs are higher, which drives up insurance rates. People miss work when they or their family members are sick. That reduces productivity. If someone does not recover, society misses out on that person's potential economic and social contributions.

Superbug infections occur outside the United States too. Indeed, the problem is far worse in other countries. Quality medical care is not always available. Even when it is, poverty often prevents people from getting effective treatment.

High rates of malaria in Africa and TB in Russia are just two examples where drug resistance is out of control. The potential implications are dire.

"Once life-saving medicines are increasingly having as little effect as a sugar pill," warned the World Health Organization in 2000. "Microbial resistance to treatment could bring the world back to a pre-antibiotic age."[18]

Rates of drug-resistant disease are on the rise. Look at *Streptococcus pneumoniae*. Among other things, the bacteria can cause pneumonia, ear infections, and even meningitis (swelling of the brain's lining). By 2004, up to 40 percent of strep cases could probably resist at least two antibiotics.[19]

The higher resistance rates go, the less likely it is that the first-choice antibiotic will cure an infection. In those cases, patients need other antibiotics. Heavier use of such antibiotics puts more selective pressure on bacteria to develop resistance to those drugs. Patients then need other drugs. At some point, even drugs of last resort may not work.

People used to see antibiotics as sure cures for disease. Antibiotics still cure most patients with bacterial diseases. More and more, though, doctors cannot always count on the first-choice antibiotic for a slam-dunk cure. In the last few decades, drug-resistant diseases have become more common—and more of a public health concern.

This book explores the growing problem of drug-resistant diseases. It looks at microbes, antibiotics, and the mechanisms of resistance. It will examine how resistance has spread and developed into a significant public health problem. It highlights areas where the problem is especially acute.

This book also explores how scientists are trying to fight drug-resistant diseases. Political and legal issues come into play. Individual choices make a difference too.

Battle Against the "Bugs"

Humans rule the earth. They have built massive cities and monuments. They have produced beautiful art and music. They can communicate with each other almost anywhere on the planet. Scientists have harnessed different energy forms and probed into the mysteries of life and matter. People have even ventured into space.

Yet microbes clearly have people outnumbered. Presently, the world has about 6.4 billion people.[1] In contrast, over a billion microbes can live in a single teaspoon of soil.[2]

Tiny as they are, they can kill. Microbes are microorganisms, tiny organisms that cannot be seen with the naked eye. They are Earth's oldest life-forms—and some of the toughest, too.

Meet the Microbes

Humans' first close-up look at microbes came in 1674. Dutch merchant Antonie van Leeuwenhoek (1632–1723) looked at water through a homemade microscope. He saw tiny things moving around. He called them "wee animalcules."[3]

Most microbes are not dangerous. In fact, many are down-right useful. Bacteria and fungi break down dead organisms. That provides nutrients for new life and keeps dead organisms from piling up all around. Similarly, protists "eat" sewage at wastewater treatment plants.

Microbes can cause serious illness, though. Louis Pasteur of France (1822–1895) was one of the most vocal champions for the germ theory of disease. This is the idea that microbes cause disease. Disease-causing microbes are called pathogens.

Germany's Robert Koch (1843–1910) advanced the germ theory. In 1881, he found a way to culture, or grow, bacteria on a mixture of gelatin and agar (an algae-based material). Using this method, Koch showed that bacteria from sick animals could produce the same disease in another animal. This proved which microbes caused certain diseases. During his career, Koch also isolated the bacteria that cause cholera and tuberculosis.

Bacteria are one form of microbes. They are single-celled organisms that live, grow, and divide on their own. Bacteria cells have no separate nucleus. That sets them apart from other living things. Archaea (bacteria-like microbes found in extreme environments) are the only other living things with no separate nucleus.

Many fungi are also microbes, such as yeasts and molds. Fungal pathogens cause athlete's foot, nail infections, and other diseases. (Larger, multicelled fungi like mushrooms and toad-stools are not microbes, though.)

Protists are another type of single-celled microbes. *Giardia lamblia* causes diarrhea. *Trichomas vaginalis* causes a sexually transmitted disease. *Plasmodium* parasites cause malaria.

Viruses differ dramatically from other microbes. Technically, they are not even alive, because they cannot reproduce on their own. Viruses are basically packages of genetic material with a structure for attacking living cells. Until viruses attach to such cells, called hosts, they do not do anything.

Once viral pathogens enter host cells, however, they take over. The host cells become factories for making more viruses. Eventually, the host cells break open and die. That releases more viruses to attack more cells. Because of viruses' unique structure, medicines that work against bacteria or fungi have no effect on them.

A prion is another type of pathogen that does not live on its own. Prions are abnormal forms of proteins. They infect organisms and convert normal proteins into more prions. With Creutzfeldt-Jakob disease (CJD), prions target proteins needed for the nervous system to work right. Over time, they interfere with normal brain functions and destroy muscle coordination. Transmission of CJD is a major reason why health officials worry about mad cow disease in beef.

Bacteria Basics

Because antibiotic resistance is a huge problem, it helps to take a closer look at bacteria and antibiotics. Bacteria are probably the most numerous living things on Earth. Tens of thousands of species exist, and any effort to count them would be almost fruitless. Estimates say more than 3.9×10^{23} (1, followed by 23 zeroes) bacteria live just in people's guts. Counting the billions of bacteria in soil, water, and air would boost the number much higher.[4]

Bacteria's single DNA chromosome floats freely inside the cell's cytoplasm. Sometimes bacteria also have little extra rings of DNA, called plasmids. Sometimes that DNA affects the cell's traits.

Ribosomes put together proteins that the cell needs. Each cell requires thousands of proteins to function properly. For example, cells need to take in food and metabolize it. They get rid of wastes. Cells control the amount of water and salts inside them. They grow and divide. Virtually everything the cell does requires proteins made by the ribosomes.

Scientists classify bacteria based on their shapes. Cocci are generally round, or spherical. Bacilli are rod shaped. Spirilla or spirochetes are spiral-shaped, like a comma or corkscrew.

Scientists also group bacteria by whether they hold a purple gram stain. Danish scientist Hans Christian Gram (1853–1938) worked out the method in the late 1880s. Bacteria that absorb the purple dye are gram-positive. Bacteria that do not hold the stain are gram-negative.

Gram's technique made it easier for scientists to see and study certain bacteria. It also gave clues about bacteria's cell wall structures. Gram-positive bacteria have just a single cell wall. Gram-negative bacteria have multiple cell wall layers, so it is harder for the purple stain to get in.

Compared to other life-forms, bacteria are pretty simple. But their life processes can be complex. Look at how bacteria get their genetic traits. Bacteria have a single chromosome made of DNA (deoxyribonucleic acid). At a molecular level, DNA resembles a twisted ladder. The arrangement of chemical groups along that twisted ladder determines most of the cell's traits.

When bacteria reproduce, their chromosomal DNA untwists, and the twisted-ladder shape comes apart. Based on the genetic code, each half of the twisted-ladder molecule makes the complementary nucleic acid groups that would make up the ladder's other half. The new DNA molecules then move to opposite sides of the cell.

The cell wall pinches in at the middle and forms a new wall.

Now two daughter cells have the same traits as the first cell. This process is called cell division. Some bacteria repeat this cycle every twenty minutes.

Bacterial DNA does not always stay the same, however. By chance, the DNA can change, or mutate, during cell division. That produces a relatively permanent change, or mutation, that the organism can pass on to other generations. Harmful mutations interfere with the cell's normal functioning. Useful mutations help the cell survive.

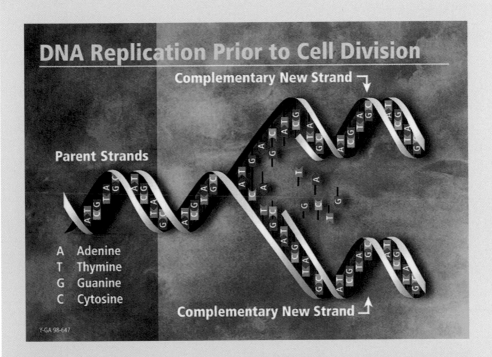

DNA Replication Prior to Cell Division

Complementary New Strand

Parent Strands

A Adenine
T Thymine
G Guanine
C Cytosine

Y-GA 98-647

Complementary New Strand

Each time a cell divides into two daughter cells, its full genome is duplicated. During cell division, the DNA molecule unwinds and the weak bonds between the base pairs break, allowing the strands to separate. Each daughter cell receives one old and one new DNA strand.
Source: U.S. Department of Energy Human Genome Program, "U.S. DOE Genome Image Gallery," n.d., <http://www.ornl.gove/hgmis> (March 8, 2005).

Bacteria have other ways of getting DNA too. In a process called *conjugation*, one bacterium hooks onto another and forms a tube, called a pilus. The first cell then gives a copy of its plasmid DNA to the other. The other cell is not always in the same species as the first.

Bacteria can also pick up stray bits of DNA from their environment, perhaps left over from dead cells. Other times, a type of virus called a bacteriophage, or phage, infects the bacteria. If the phage is a type that does not kill its host, new DNA becomes part of the chromosome. The cell passes on that DNA when it reproduces.

These traits help bacteria evolve in response to changes in their environment. Bacteria have other survival tricks too. Some bacteria form spores for when they go into resting cycles. Those spores can often survive harsh conditions. Later, the bacteria can become active again.

Biofilms also help bacteria survive. Slimelike biofilms attach lots of bacteria to a surface and protect the colony. The sticky feeling of morning mouth is one example.

Some biofilm-forming bacteria cause serious disease. *Pseudomonas aeruginosa* forms biofilms in the lungs. That can give cystic fibrosis patients pneumonia. The same genes that cause the bacteria to make biofilms also help them resist antibiotics.[5]

Bacteria have existed on Earth for billions of years. Today they are evading some of humans' most powerful weapons against disease.

The Antibiotic Age Begins

Antibiotics kill or limit the growth of bacteria. Originally, scientists used the term just for antibacterial medicines derived from natural sources. Now many antibiotics are partly or fully man-made. Antimicrobials are a broader group. They include both lab-made and natural agents to kill or limit any microbes.

Antibiotics have existed in nature for millions of years. Some organisms secrete the substances to keep other microbes from moving in on their "turf." That cuts down on competition for space and food.

Some ancient cultures may have used such natural antibiotics. Psalm 51 in the Bible talks about cleansing with hyssop. A fungus that often grows with the plant makes a form of penicillin.[6] Central American natives treated infections with molds too.[7]

After scientists accepted the germ theory of diseases, they began looking for substances to kill bacteria. In 1888, German scientist Edouard de Freudenreich discovered that *Pseudomonas aeruginosa* secreted something that killed other bacteria. But the substance was toxic and unstable.

Another German scientist, Paul Ehrlich (1854–1915), felt convinced that a "magic bullet" could kill bacteria without harming people. Working with Japanese scientist Sahachiro Hata (1873–1938), he developed Salvarsan. That arsenic-linked dye worked as an antibacterial, but it had serious side effects. Still, scientists did not give up hope.

In 1928, Alexander Fleming (1881–1955) was a researcher at St. Mary's Hospital in London. After a weekend away, Fleming found a mess in his lab. A fluffy mass of mold covered his culture plates of *Staphylococcus aureus* bacteria.

Maybe the spores came in through an airshaft. Maybe they got in through a window. Either way, Fleming's cultures were ruined. He cleared away the plates to clean and disinfect them. When a colleague stopped by, Fleming showed him one of the plates.

At that point, Fleming noticed something odd. The area on the plate around the mold was transparent. Something had killed the bacteria that were there.[8]

Fleming began experimenting. The mold, *Penicillium notatum*, secreted a yellowish fluid that he called penicillin. It killed not just staph, but also other types of gram-positive bacteria. It had less effect on gram-negative bacteria.

Even better, penicillin was not toxic. It could kill bacteria without major harm to animals. Fleming published his discovery in 1929.[9]

Penicillin seemed like the long-sought "magic bullet." But there was a catch. Scientists needed a way to make pure penicillin for medicinal use. Working in England, Howard Florey (1898–1968) and Ernst Chain (1906–1979) tackled this problem.

In late 1940, Florey and Chain injected their penicillin into a forty-eight-year-old London policeman. The man was very sick with blood poisoning from staph. By the third day, the patient's fever came down. The penicillin was working. Sadly, the supply ran out after five days. The infection grew and spread again, and the patient died.[10]

Florey and Chain knew their penicillin worked. Now they needed a way to make it in large quantities. Needing more money, they turned to the United States. With World War II on the horizon, the government agreed to help. Penicillin could be a major weapon against wound infections on the battlefield.

During 1941 and 1942, doctors got permission to give penicillin to a few patients where no other medicine could help. The medicine saved lives, but few people knew about penicillin. That was about to change.

Alexander Fleming, the discoverer of penicillin, wrote on this petri dish he used in the laboratory. Fleming's discovery was to save millions of lives, but strains of bacteria resistant to the wonder drug were quick to emerge.

On November 28, 1942, over eight hundred people crowded into a Boston nightclub called The Cocoanut Grove. Suddenly, a fake palm tree caught fire. The flames quickly jumped up and spread. The panicked crowd tried to escape, and many people became trapped. Over 450 people died. Hundreds more suffered severe burns.

Third-degree burns are painful. They get infected easily too. Traveling with a police escort, a truck drove from New Jersey to Massachusetts General Hospital. On board were 32 liters of penicillin. Thanks to the delivery, hundreds of victims survived. The story made headlines across the country.[11]

> **Penicillin seemed like the long-sought "magic bullet"—something that could kill bacteria without harming the people who took it.**

By autumn of 1943, penicillin was helping soldiers in combat zones.[12] As hoped, penicillin worked wonders on the battlefields of World War II. One 1944 ad showed a medic helping an injured soldier. "Thanks to PENICILLIN . . . He Will Come Home," it said.[13]

An Era of Wonder Drugs

While Florey's team worked on penicillin, other medical advances took place too. In the late 1930s, sulfonamides—commonly called sulfa drugs—became the first synthetically made antimicrobial. Sulfonamides still help treat diseases like bronchitis, skin infections, and urinary tract infections.

The work of Selman Waksman (1888–1973) yielded more milestones. Waksman and his team knew that soil harbors thousands of types of microbes. Thus, they searched through over ten thousand cultures of soil microbes. Their work led to nearly two dozen antibiotics. In 1944, Waksman developed streptomycin from *Streptococcus griseus*. The antibiotic became the first drug to treat tuberculosis successfully. It could also cure urinary tract infections, meningitis, and tularemia ("rabbit fever"). Waksman won a Nobel Prize for his work in 1952.[14]

By the 1960s, doctors had a whole array of antibacterial drugs. Different medicines target specific features of bacteria.

How do antibacterial drugs work? Some drugs interfere with bacteria's cell wall. For example, Beta-lactam antibiotics prevent

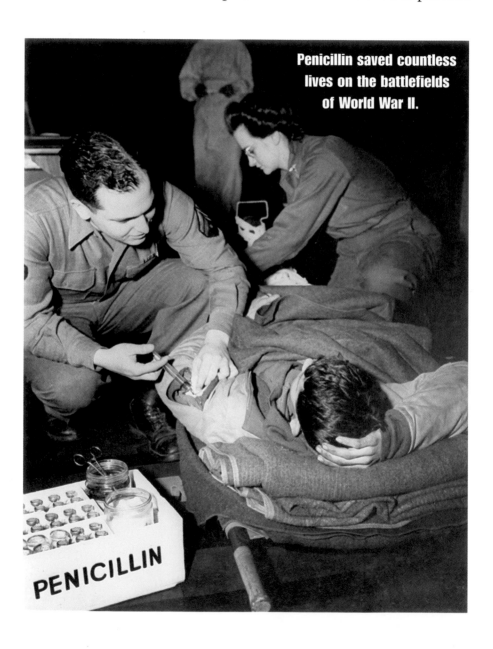

Penicillin saved countless lives on the battlefields of World War II.

PENICILLIN

bacteria from making more peptidoglycan, a main component in cell walls. If the bacteria cannot build a new cell wall after division, they die. Penicillin and cephalosporins work this way.

Other drugs affect bacteria's cell membrane—a layer between the cell wall and the cell's insides. Polymycins and amphotericin ß fall into this category.

Still other drugs interfere with bacteria's ribosomes. They keep the cell from making proteins it needs to survive. Tetracyclines and erythromycin work this way.

Antibiotics and other antibacterial drugs can target other cell functions too. Quinolones and nalidixic acid interfere with the way that the cell puts DNA together. Rifampin targets mRNA, which is a chemical that carries instructions to the ribosomes for making proteins. Sulfonamides target folate synthesis in the cell.[15]

In short, antimicrobials work by attacking specific parts or functions of bacterial cells. The flip side of this is that the drugs will not work if a microbe does not have the targeted structure or perform a certain function. *Thus, antibiotics do not work on viruses.*

Bacteria Fight Back

Antibiotic-resistant bacteria exist in nature, but they were relatively rare until the antibiotic age. Bacteria had limited exposure to natural antibiotics. Plus, resistance genes carry some biological costs. In other words, it costs bacteria cells something to be resistant to antibiotics. The resistant genes might use up some of the bacteria's energy, or the cells might grow or reproduce more slowly.[16] All else being equal, the susceptible strains have an advantage over strains with natural antibiotic resistance.

Once the modern antibiotic age began, humans made and used large quantities of antibiotics and other antimicrobials. This shifted the balance of power in nature. Now selective pressure gave resistant forms of bacteria a competitive advantage over other strains.

In other words, the antibiotics did their job and killed susceptible bacteria. By wiping out the competition, though, the drugs would select for any resistant strains. This means that the drugs left those bacteria alive to reproduce.

Resistance to sulfonamide drugs showed up by the late 1930s. As early as 1945, Fleming himself worried about penicillin resistance. He especially worried about people taking too-small doses in pill form. Then, he warned, the microbes might be "educated to resist penicillin."[17] René Dubos (1901–1982) at the Rockefeller Institute had similar fears.[18]

Just as antibiotics attack bacteria in specific ways, bacteria fight back with different tricks. These mechanisms start out as random mutations. Bacteria can also swap resistance genes through conjugation. The genes give the bacteria traits to survive an antibiotic attack. Indeed, bacteria that can resist one type of antibiotic often can resist others too.

Sometimes the bacteria disguise themselves. They change the targets where an antibiotic would attach to the cells. Many penicillin-resistant bacteria work this way. Such a trick also helps bacteria resist drugs like rifampin and erythromycin.

Adding extra bits onto the antibiotic molecule is another technique. That changes the antibiotic's shape so it cannot attach to the bacteria. Some bacteria that resist streptomycin, neomycin, and kanamycin do this.

Another resistance trick is to break down the antibiotic. Some resistant staph strains make an enzyme to break down part of penicillin called the ß-lactam ring. To deal with this, scientists developed methicillin—a chemically altered form of penicillin. But now some bacteria can resist that drug too.

Other bacteria have substitute enzymes to save them. Some bacteria that resist trimethoprim and sulfonamides use a different enzyme to do the job the antibiotics would otherwise prevent. As an analogy, if you had your own backup generator, a blackout in the neighborhood would not cut off your power.

Some bacteria get rid of antimicrobials with efflux pumps. Just as vomiting can get rid of something that upsets the stomach, efflux pumps remove antimicrobial drugs so they cannot hurt the bacteria. Some strains that resist tetracycline work this way.

Not only can bacteria become resistant to antibiotics, but some strains even grow to depend on them. In 2004, researchers at the University of Wisconsin reported three cases of vancomycin-dependent *Enterococcus* infections.[19] Apparently, prolonged exposure to that drug plus other antibiotics encouraged the growth of strains that thrived in the drugs' presence. Vancomycin has been the drug of last resort, so this type of drug resistance is especially scary.

Defeating drug-resistant bacteria often calls for new drugs that get around the germs' resistance mechanisms. But then selective pressure encourages development of bacteria that can resist the new medicine too. In the battle against the superbugs, medical experts are racing to stay one step ahead.

Beyond Bacteria

Much of the attention on drug-resistant diseases focuses on bacteria. More medicines exist to kill or disable disease-causing bacteria. That puts selective pressure on bacteria to develop resistance.

Bacteria are not the only microbes that become resistant to drugs. Viruses can also mutate and evolve. Antiviral drugs for flu became common only within the last decade. Yet already some flu strains show resistance. In one study, nearly 20 percent of children with flu who were treated with an antiviral drug developed resistant strains of the virus.[20] Even with vaccines, preventing an epidemic of drug-resistant flu could be tough.

Other types of microbes can evolve to resist drugs as well.

Chapter 5 looks at the dilemma of drug-resistant HIV, which is caused by a virus. It also examines the menace of malaria. That disease results when an infected mosquito transmits a parasite.

Ongoing research will give more clues about how microbes become resistant to drugs. Those clues can help experts design new medicines. Meanwhile, the more people can do to curb the rise in drug-resistant disease, the better everyone will be.

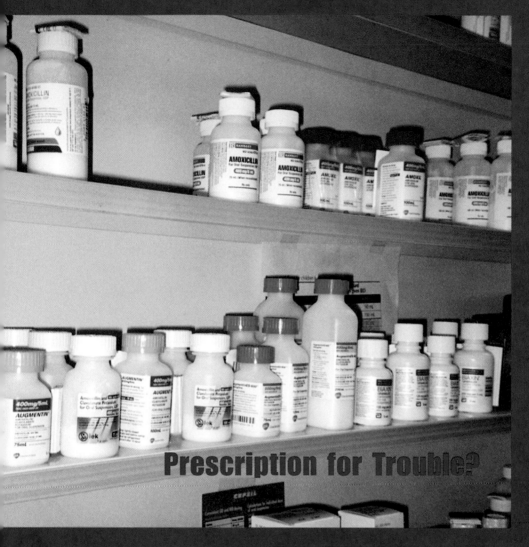

Back in the 1950s and 1960s, people saw antibiotics as "miracle drugs."[1] Now there is no such thing as a sure cure.

Any antibiotic use can select for drug-resistant bacteria. When antibiotics cure disease, some risk may be all right. But misuse and overuse of these medicines make the problem worse.

Miracle Medicines?

In 1954, U.S. companies made 2 million pounds of antibiotics. By 1998, the total was over 50 million pounds.[2] About 126 million antibiotic prescriptions each year go to outpatients—people who do not stay in the hospital.[3] That comes to about 80 percent of the total human use in the United States.[4] As discussed later, animals use antibiotics too.

In treating patients, doctors can choose many different antibiotics. Some have only a few uses. Others, like amoxycillin and penicillin, are broad-spectrum medicines. That means that they fight a wide range of infections.

By and large, antibiotics do a great job. The medical community relies on them. The public does too—perhaps too much. In one survey, nearly half of all patients said they expect to get antibiotics if they feel sick enough to see the doctor.[5]

The Centers for Disease Control and Prevention (CDC) has estimated that up to a third of the antibiotics that Americans take each year may be prescribed improperly.[6] Patients may get antibiotics when they do not need them. Or, patients may get an antibiotic that is not right for their sickness.

Viruses cause many illnesses, and antibiotics do nothing against them. Bacteria and viruses differ in their basic structures. Viruses just do not have the structures and functions that antibiotics attack.

Despite that, many people want antibiotics for whatever ails them. They may not understand the differences between viruses and bacteria. Or they may want antibiotics, "just in case." Sometimes people feel better after they take anything—even a pill that contains no medication—just because they expect to feel better. Scientists call this the placebo effect. (*Placebo* is from a Latin word meaning "to please," and it refers to a substance, such as a sugar pill, taken by test subjects in place of a real medicine for comparison purposes in a study.) But sugar pills do not have significant biological effects. Antibiotics do.

Beyond this, patients often do not take antibiotics as directed. Some people stop taking them too soon. Others skip multiple doses.

"People often think that once they start to feel better, they should stop taking their antibiotics. That's not something that they should do," notes Richard Besser. He heads the Get Smart: Know When Antibiotics Work program at the CDC. "We think it's important that people take their entire course of antibiotics so that their infection is truly killed and doesn't come back."[7]

If people stop taking their antibiotics too early, the remaining bacteria get a chance to regroup. Without the antibiotic fighting them, they multiply. The patient feels sick again—maybe worse than before. But now most of the bacteria can resist the first antibiotic. The patient then needs a different medicine, which may not work as well.

As an analogy, think of bacteria as boats at sea. If antibiotics punch holes in the bottom, the bacteria need to work to bail water so they do not sink. The full dose of antibiotics will keep doing damage to the bacteria until they can no longer bail out seawater. With too little antibiotics, though, the bacteria could feel like they have just had a great workout and come back stronger.

Another common error is taking leftover antibiotics from an earlier illness. Sharing leftover antibiotics with family members is also a bad idea. The pills may not work against the present illness. Even if they did, there would not be enough doses to kill the infection.

People also think antibiotics can keep a cold from getting worse. That mistaken belief "is a good way to select for a resistant infection," says Besser.[8] Antibiotics do not fight colds, because viruses cause colds. Meanwhile, fighting the cold already taxes the immune system. With other bacteria out of the way and the body's defenses lowered, resistant bacteria can multiply and cause more sickness.

What Harm Can It Do?

For a long time, doctors in the United States and Canada freely gave antibiotics to patients. People can still get antibiotics "over the counter"—that is, without a prescription—in many parts of Africa, Asia, and Latin America.

In many cases, the antibiotics seemed to help. Even if they did not, side effects were often mild. Taking extra medicine did not seem like it could hurt.

Experiences with drug-resistant disease have shown otherwise. The more antibiotics people take, the more selective pressure there is for bacteria to develop resistance. And improper use of antibiotics makes it easier for that to happen.

A normal, healthy person has millions of bacteria in or on the body. For the most part, those bacteria are benign, or not harmful. Many bacteria even help with normal bodily functions, like digestion.

When someone takes an antibiotic, the medicine does not know which are the good bacteria and which are the bad. The medicine just attacks all the bacteria it can. This is especially true for broad-spectrum antibiotics.

The antibiotics treat the disease, but they also wipe out many harmless and even helpful bacteria. The normal flora—the generally benign bacteria that usually exist in the system—eventually build back up. Meanwhile, patients can have problems.

According to the Centers for Disease Control, up to one third of the antibiotics taken by Americans each year may be prescribed improperly.

Some people get diarrhea from not having those good bacteria around. Some people also develop diarrhea because resistant bacteria get a clear field to thrive. *Clostridium difficile* causes 15 to 25 percent of antibiotic-associated diarrhea cases, says the CDC.[9]

Antibiotics can leave the field clear for other infections too. As long as they are there, benign bacteria usually outcompete harmful ones for space and food. Wiping out the healthy microbes removes that competition. Pathogens then have a better chance to multiply out of control and cause sickness.

Salmonella poisoning comes from food tainted with the live bacteria. In a significant number of cases, people who get *Salmonella* have recently taken antibiotics for something else. Those patients probably do not have their normal flora back yet. Otherwise, those microbes might have crowded out the invading bacteria.[10]

Even if someone does not get sick right away, resistant bacteria may eventually invade other parts of the body. Bacteria from the intestines sometimes cause painful urinary tract infections (UTIs). Each year, one in nine American women suffers from a UTI. While antibiotics cure most UTIs, drug resistance has become more common in recent years.[11]

Enterococcus infections are also a growing problem. As long as *Enterococcus faecium* and *Enterococcus faecilis* stay in the digestive tract, they usually do not make people sick. When people's immune systems weaken, the bacteria may multiply out of control and spread. This is a particular risk for hospital patients or people with certain diseases.

Drug-resistant *Enterococcus* infections are a serious problem for hospital patients and people with certain diseases. The first cases showed up in England and France in 1987, and the first U.S. case appeared in 1989. By 2000, the United States had about seventy-five hundred cases of vancomycin-resistant *Enterococcus* (VRE) each year.[12] Without strict disease control measures, infections can spread quickly, especially in hospital wards.

Resistant germs do not necessarily stay in institutions either. Visitors or staff can inadvertently spread infections. Also, many patients have shorter hospital stays than people did twenty or thirty years ago. That increases the chances of bringing resistant bacteria home.

Wherever a resistance gene emerges, it can spread to other bacteria. Plus, resistance to one antibiotic seems to encourage bacteria to resist multiple drugs.[13] In part, the mechanism that lets the bacteria resist one drug could work on others too. Plus, resistance

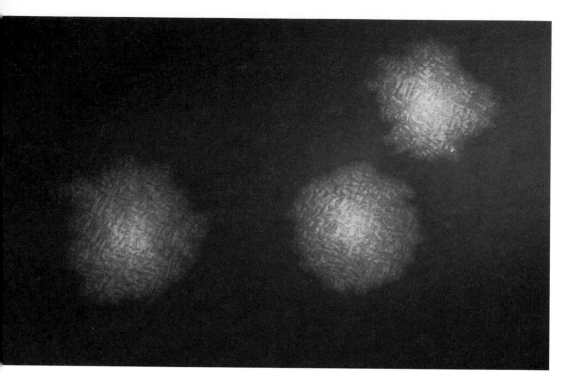

Clostridium difficile colonies grown in a lab. This bacteria causes
15 to 25 percent of diarrhea associated with antibiotic use.

genes on plasmids often transfer from bacteria to bacteria as
"packages." Those resistance gene packages often carry a host of
traits that can fight a variety of drugs.

"As more and more bacteria of different kinds become resistant, then it limits the kinds of drugs that we have," notes Stuart
B. Levy at Tufts University and the Alliance for the Prudent Use
of Antibiotics.[14] When bacteria resist half a dozen or more
antibiotics, doctors may run out of options. Patients may be left
without a cure and with little hope for survival.

Impatient Outpatients and Other Problems

Doctors know overuse of antibiotics adds to the problem of
drug resistance. Yet they have not always practiced what experts
preach.

In one study during the 1990s, all the pediatricians surveyed said they gave patients antibiotics more often than needed. Many felt they could cut antibiotic prescriptions between 20 and 50 percent.[15] In other words, up to half the prescriptions were unnecessary.

Most of these doctors were competent professionals. They used their best judgment to choose treatments. But sometimes other factors came into play.

Pressure from patients is common. Outpatients—people who do not stay in the hospital—visit the doctor because they feel sick. And they want to feel better—now.

"Surveys show that a large proportion of Americans do not know that there's a difference between bacterial and viral infections," says Richard Besser at the CDC.[16] People want to feel better. To them, that means antibiotics.

Frustration plays in too. Patients who feel miserable may get upset if the doctor says they have "just a virus."

"Just because your doctor doesn't give you an antibiotic doesn't mean that you're not sick," stresses Besser. "Many viral infections make people feel a lot worse than they do with a bacterial infection. It's just that the treatment and the approach to it must be different."[17]

Worry factors in too. Parents want their children to feel better fast. Often, they push to get antibiotics, even if a viral infection is more likely. Parents may also feel doctors do not fully explain why antibiotics might not be a good idea.[18]

Often, doctors cannot tell right away if an infection is bacterial or viral. A 75 percent chance that an infection is viral would leave a 25 percent chance that it is bacterial.[19] Some doctors may give an antibiotic just to be on the safe side.

Beyond this, managed-care programs aim to reduce the number of patient visits. They want to limit the time that doctors spend with patients too. That works against asking someone to come back later if he or she still feels ill.[20]

Malpractice claims are a worry too. What if an infection diagnosed as viral was bacterial after all? If a doctor did not give antibiotics, could someone sue if he or she got sicker?[21] Misdiagnosis is a common basis for malpractice claims. Even if a doctor shows the treatment met the profession's standard of care, any lawsuit still brings litigation costs. Those costs, in turn, can drive up malpractice insurance costs for the profession.

Better and faster diagnostic tools could help. Look at how doctors diagnose strep throat. Viruses cause most throat infections. Group A Strep, *Streptococcus pyogenes*, causes only about 20 percent.[22] A quick throat culture test can detect that bacteria with about 95 percent accuracy. If the test is positive for strep, doctors can give antibiotics. Otherwise, doctors refrain from prescribing antibiotics. In some cases, they may also double-check the rapid test results with a follow-up lab test that takes longer but has even more reliability.

Better tests for other types of bacteria would tell doctors if other sicknesses were bacterial instead of viral. They could also help doctors target infections with specific antibiotics instead of broad-spectrum drugs.[23] Right now, though, one cannot easily get samples from patients' ears or lungs and test them while people wait.

Earaches can be a big pain—and a big factor in overuse of antibiotics. As of 2004, about half of all preschool children's antibiotic prescriptions were for earaches. Viruses cause most children's earaches. When bacteria are the culprits, *Streptococcus pneumoniae* is often at fault.

Despite the odds, children often received antibiotics for earaches. From 1996 to 1999, penicillin-resistant strep rates went from 22 percent to 27 percent. Rates of erythromycin-resistant strep nearly doubled, from 11 percent to 20 percent.[24]

Even when bacteria do cause earaches, 80 percent of children will feel better within three days—whether they take antibiotics or not.[25] Thus, in 2004, the American Academy of Pediatrics issued new guidelines.[26]

For most children over six months old, the guidelines recommend a "wait-and-see" approach. Doctors and parents take steps to relieve the child's pain. Meanwhile, they let the child's immune system battle the infection. If children do not feel better within a few days, doctors look at the case again. Children might then get amoxycillin or another antibiotic.

Delayed prescriptions are another tool. Doctors can recommend steps to relieve pain and other symptoms. Patients might get an antibiotic prescription too. But the doctor would tell them to use it only if they still feel awful after several days.

For such approaches to work, patients need to know why they should wait. They should also feel comfortable about checking back with their doctors if they do not get better soon. Good communication between doctors and patients is essential.

After all, patients go to the doctor because they want to feel better. If they take medicine, they want to feel better faster than if they took nothing. If there is little difference, why risk side effects and apply selective pressure for drug resistance?

"We treat diseases, not bacteria," stresses John Powers, head of Antimicrobial Drug Development and Resistance Initiatives at the Food and Drug Administration (FDA).[27] In other words, the crucial issue is what will make a person feel better. That is far more important than whether the patient walks out of the doctor's office with a prescription for antibiotics or other drugs.

Fortunately, things are looking up. From 1990 to 2000, the CDC saw a 40 percent decline in antibiotic prescriptions for children by office-based doctors.[28] Antimicrobial prescriptions in hospitals' ambulatory care (walk-in) facilities dropped by about 25 percent between 1992 and 2000.[29]

"Anecdotally, we're hearing from doctors that patients are starting to reframe their question," says Besser at the CDC. Instead of just asking for an antibiotic, many people now ask if

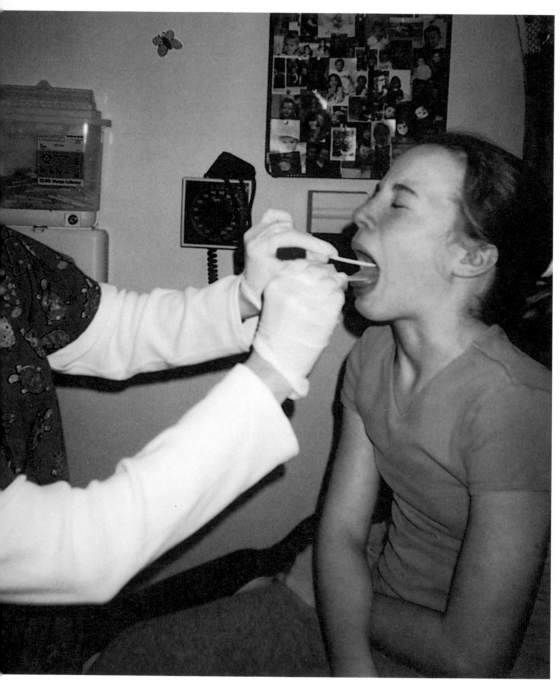

A quick test can tell whether a sore throat is caused by strep or not. A negative strep test means that something else—most likely a virus—is the culprit.

they need one. "It takes a lot of pressure off of the physician so that they are more comfortable prescribing appropriately."[30]

Battling Bugs at the Hospital

Most drug-resistant diseases still occur at hospitals and other health care institutions. These are the biggest battlegrounds for fighting superbugs.

Hospital patients are especially vulnerable to resistant infections. They are already weak from whatever illness or injury they came in with. Fighting off another infection is hard.

Hospitals use lots of antibiotics and antimicrobial products. The medicines do their job. But they also apply selective pressure. They kill susceptible strains of bacteria. But then resistant bacteria can thrive.

Health care workers can also spread infections from person to person. In theory, all staff should clean their hands between patients. In practice, the CDC found that health care workers took all recommended steps less than half the time.[31] Some people felt they had too little time during long workdays. Others worried about getting chapped hands. Still others were just careless.

Educating staff and posting reminders promote better hand washing. Supervisors must give feedback too. Patient education also helps. Staff people feel embarrassed if patients catch them cutting corners.

Making cleanup more convenient helps a lot. Nonirritating alcohol-based wipes have become very popular. Also, some hospitals have hand cleanser dispensers outside patient rooms for health care workers and visitors.

When hospitals improve hand hygiene and take other steps, patient infection rates drop. In two studies, infant-care units that improved hygiene practices had no MRSA cases afterward for the entire time researchers studied those facilities. In another study, a hospital cut its VRE infection rate by 85 percent.[32]

Screening patients can help too. If doctors know that someone already carries certain resistant bacteria, they are one step ahead. Isolating patients with certain diseases, such as VRE, helps too.[33]

Prescribing different medicines sometimes curbs selective pressure for resistant strains to develop. Thus, some patients with a disease get one antibiotic, while others get different ones. The idea is that there will not be a strong advantage for any one resistant strain. The appropriate approach depends on the setting, the type of infection, and the risks and benefits of different drugs.

In some cases, hospitals may require extra authorization from department heads or other supervisors before letting patients get certain drugs.[34] Other proposals would have government impose more restrictions on antibiotic prescriptions.[35]

On the Lookout

Monitoring drug-resistant disease is crucial in both the hospital setting and the community. Drug-resistant diseases are a problem at both the national and global levels. But the problem is also very local in nature.

"All environments have resistance problems, but it may present itself differently," explains Stuart B. Levy at Tufts University.[36] For example, Ohio may have higher rates of drug-resistant *Pneumococcus*, while Iowa might have higher rates of MRSA. Resistance rates for diseases also vary from country to country.

Monitoring programs collect data about what diseases occur and where. The programs aim to spot public health problems before they become a crisis. Many bacteria like staph and strep live almost everywhere. If most infections in an area remain susceptible, then doctors can cure most cases with antibiotics.

As resistance rates rise, patients run a greater risk that the first-choice antibiotic will not work. In contrast, a drop in rates can show how different steps might reduce drug-resistant diseases.

Keep Antibiotics Working

Overuse and misuse of antibiotics are not the only reasons why drug-resistant diseases occur. Indeed, most experts feel bacteria would eventually become resistant to antibiotics anyway. After all, chance mutations happen in nature. But human actions have sped up the rise in drug-resistant disease.

Keep Antibiotics Working is a coalition that includes the Alliance for the Prudent Use of Antibiotics, the Union of Concerned Scientists, and other groups. The CDC and FDA also have active programs to curb unnecessary use of antibiotics. WHO is involved in global efforts too.

Almost no one wants people to stop using antibiotics altogether. Rather, most experts want doctors to prescribe the drugs wisely. And they want patients to take the medicines only as directed. That way, everyone has a better chance that these important medicines will work when they are really needed.

"The spread of resistant organisms is almost part and parcel of using antibiotics. It's almost unavoidable," says John Powers at the FDA. "But you can slow it down by not using the drugs when you don't need to use them."[37]

Pediatrics estimated that animal antibiotic use made up between 40 and 80 percent of the total.[7]

In contrast, a 2001 report by the Union of Concerned Scientists put the figure used for growth promoters around 24.6 million pounds per year. That was eight times more than the 3 million pounds of antibiotics that people used for medical purposes.[8]

Stuart B. Levy at Tufts University estimates that U.S. farmers use 15 to 17 million pounds of growth promoters each year. That would be up to 80 percent of the total antibiotics used for animals.[9] "They're good, old-fashioned antibiotics being used at less than their therapeutic amounts, but they still can select for resistance," warns Levy.[10]

The Animal Health Institute is an industry group for makers of animal drugs. It says growth promoters make up only 13 percent of all antibiotics used in the United States. The remaining 87 percent would go to treat or prevent disease in people or animals.[11] Whichever estimate one picks, growth promoter use still comes to millions of pounds of antibiotics.

Fruits and vegetables sometimes get antibiotics too. For example, farmers spray streptomycin on apple or pear trees to prevent a disease called blight. Oxytetracycline is another antibiotic used in growing peaches, pears, and nectarines.[12] Washing can remove these from the food chain, although the chemicals might then get into wastewater treatment systems.

Playing Chicken?

Just as when people take them, animal-use antibiotics can select for resistant bacteria. How might that affect rates of drug-resistant disease?

For years, poultry farmers used certain drugs, called fluoroquinolones, to control outbreaks of harmful *E. coli* and *Pasteurella multocida.* The poultry drugs worked, but many chickens developed drug-resistant *Campylobacter.* The bacteria

Many farmers feed low doses of antibiotics to livestock as growth promoters.

do not make birds sick, but they can cause serious diarrhea in people.

Ciprofloxacin, or Cipro, usually treats the disease. However, Cipro is in the same class as the poultry drugs. Potentially, bacteria that could resist the poultry drugs used the same mechanism to resist Cipro.

Rates of drug-resistant *Campylobacter jejuni* infections rose from 13 percent in 1997 to 19 percent in 2001.[13] Those people stayed sick longer, with an average of twelve days of diarrhea, versus six for other cases.[14] Studies linked the increase in drug resistance to the poultry drugs.[15]

In 2000, the FDA recommended a ban on poultry farmers' use of fluoroquinolones. Abbott Laboratories voluntarily took its drug off the market, but Bayer officials resisted.

The next year, terrorists sent deadly anthrax bacteria through the mail. Cipro was doctors' drug of choice for treating exposed people. Health experts like Ellen K. Silbergeld at the University of Maryland and Polly Walker at Johns Hopkins University became worried about what would happen if Cipro stopped working.[16] If poultry drug use could promote higher rates of drug-resistant *Campylobacter jejuni*, plasmid transfer or other mechanisms could potentially give anthrax bacteria the ability to fight off Cipro too.

Cries to ban animal antibiotics in the same class as Cipro grew. In March 2004, the FDA withdrew its approval for Bayer's poultry drug.[17] That addressed one concern. But it left open other questions about the farm industry's use of antibiotics.

Salmonella is another foodborne disease. Since the late 1960s, some scientists worried that animals could pass on drug-resistant strains to people. In Great Britain, rates of drug-resistant *Salmonella* dropped after a ban on various growth promoters in the same class as human drugs.[18]

In 1998, a twelve-year-old Nebraska boy became sick with abdominal pain, fever, and diarrhea. His case of *Salmonella* resisted both ceftriaxone and ceftiofur. Molecular analysis showed that his *Salmonella* came from cattle.[19]

Indeed, *Salmonella* bacteria often show up in meat. One study analyzed two hundred ground meat samples from supermarkets around Washington, D.C. Twenty percent of the samples had the bacteria. Eighty-four percent of the strains resisted at least one antibiotic. Half of them resisted three or more antibiotics.[20]

More sanitary processing conditions can control bacteria in meat to some extent. Irradiation can kill bacteria too, although such processes raise some controversy.[21] Consumers can more easily avoid problems by handling foods properly and cooking meats thoroughly. Yet the risk of bacterial contamination cannot be fully eliminated.

Specific diseases are not the only worry. One 2003 study looked at dental plaque from eighteen young children. Most of them had tetracycline-resistant bacteria. Young children usually have not had that antibiotic. Thus, meat and fruits were the likely sources. The bacteria did not seem to make the children ill.[22] However, bacteria's ability to spread through the body and to swap resistance genes causes concern. What if those resistance genes got into *Enterococci* or other bacteria in the body that later caused disease?

Could animal antibiotics threaten the usefulness of last-resort drugs? Farmers never used vancomycin as a growth promoter. In Europe, however, farmers used the antibiotic avoparcin. That chemical's structure is similar to vancomycin.

A 1999 study in Denmark found that farm use of avoparcin created a "huge animal reservoir" of vancomycin-resistant *Enterococcus faecium* (VRE).[23] Basically, the animals' bacteria became resistant to avoparcin. The same traits let them resist vancomycin.

So far, VRE illness has been rare in the European Union. After all, *Enterococcus* bacteria usually will not make people sick

This chicken is being raised without growth promoters. When growth promoters were banned in many European countries, rates of resistant bacteria from animals fell.

unless their immune systems are weak. Yet many healthy Europeans carry the VRE. Thus, hospitals there must be on guard, or VRE could become a serious problem.[24]

Even scarier is the prospect that growth promoters can select for resistance to drugs that are not even sold yet. Rhone-Poulen Rorer spent about $400 million developing Synercid. The drug showed great promise, and the FDA approved it in 1999. In one case, it saved a sixteen-year-old gunshot victim. The Oregon girl developed MRSA after surgery, and she was allergic to vancomycin. Without Synercid, she might have died.[25]

Even before the drug hit the market, though, some bacteria could resist it. One project tested 407 chickens from twenty-six supermarkets in four states. Over half had *E. faecium* bacteria that resisted Synercid. Researchers blamed growth promoters. Farmers had given chickens a related drug, virginiamycin.[26]

In another study, all the turkeys that got virginiamycin growth promoters carried *Enterococci* that resisted that drug. The bacteria were also resistant to Synercid.[27]

The Animal Health Institute denies that animal antibiotics are a significant cause of drug-resistant disease. In its view, antibiotics prevent disease and keep animals healthy. The drugs help ensure a safe and adequate food supply, while saving farmers money.[28]

In addition, some scientists question what the evidence really shows. Yes, samples from animals may have higher rates of drug-resistant bacteria. But it is tough to prove that those bacteria cause any significant amount of disease in people.[29] After all, few people dispute that people's abuse of antibiotics affects rates of drug-resistant disease. It is very hard to prove how much worse animal-use antibiotics make the problem. Also, people can prevent many foodborne diseases by cooking meats thoroughly.

Got a Beef?

Responding to worries about drug resistance, Sweden banned numerous growth promoters in 1986. Between 1995 and 1999, other European countries followed suit. They banned various growth promoters in the same classes as drugs used in human medicine.

Rates of resistant bacteria from animals dropped dramatically. Within five years of a ban on avoparcin, rates of drug-resistant *Enterococcus* infections plunged from around 75 percent to 10 percent in Denmark.[30]

Critics of growth promoters say that the bans do not hurt farmers or animals. In one study done in Denmark, animals grew fat almost as quickly even without growth promoters. And while some animals ate more feed, meat prices in stores stayed about the same. If animals got sick, veterinarians could then give therapeutic doses of antibiotics.[31] More space, fresh air, and sunlight can keep disease rates down too.

The Animal Health Institute, in contrast, argues that bans increase disease rates among animals. After some European countries stopped using growth promoters, farms needed more antibiotics to treat sick animals than they did before. Foes of a growth promoter ban also say there is no proof it would improve people's health.[32]

So far, the U.S. government agrees that some studies show potential risks from animal-use antibiotics.[33] The FDA has withdrawn approval for Bayer's poultry drug too. Yet at least one government study questions if higher feed costs, lower production, and higher prices might follow from a general ban on growth promoters.[34] For now, agencies say they need more data before going forward with any widespread ban.

Meanwhile, bills in Congress have tried to curb or ban use of antibiotic growth promoters for animals.[35] As this book goes to press, such bills have not yet passed. For now, at least, farmers still use a range of antibiotics.

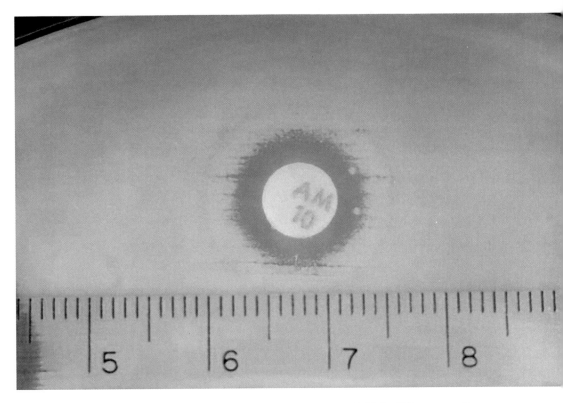

Ampicillin-resistant _E. coli_ are growing in this petri dish. This type of bacteria, often found in food, can make people deathly ill.

Some businesses are taking a stand. Large companies often do business worldwide, and some countries limit growth promoter use. Companies usually want to keep their international markets open.

In 2002, Tyson Foods, Foster Farms, and Perdue Farms said they had stopped using all or most of the antibiotics they used to feed to healthy chickens. The three companies sell over 200 million pounds of chicken per year.[36]

In June 2003, McDonald's changed its policy too. McDonald's buys over 2.5 billion pounds of meat each year. It ranks among the largest buyers of beef, pork, and chicken in the United States.[37]

McDonald's lets meat suppliers use antibiotics to treat sick animals and to prevent disease, but only if a veterinarian okays it. The policy forbids any use of antibiotics solely for growth promotion if drugs are in the same classes as human medicines.

Scientific studies have a big impact on how government regulates industry. Yet market forces have a huge impact too. The story is still unfolding.

The Antibacterial Craze

Antibacterial products seem to be everywhere. Supermarkets, drugstores, and department stores sell antibacterial soaps, body washes, and hand sanitizers. There are antibacterial toothpastes and mouthwashes too. Cleansers, wipes, and sprays promise to kill germs in the kitchen, bathroom, and elsewhere. Cutting boards, sponges, and even toys tout the antibacterial label.

People have used the active ingredients in these products for over thirty years. Many products contain a chemical called triclosan. Other antibacterial chemicals are quaternary ammonium compounds and triclocarban—the active ingredient in deodorant bar soaps.

In general, these chemicals kill a range of bacteria and some fungi. Triclosan works well against many gram-positive bacteria. Triclocarban especially targets the bacteria that cause body odor.

Antibacterial products sound like a good idea. After all, germs can cause disease. Sometimes they produce awful smells too. Going germ-free should reduce those problems, right? Some experts disagree.

Disinfectants like alcohol and bleach evaporate after use. But triclosan and similar products leave a film behind. They keep working to keep microbes from growing back. This helps a lot in hospitals and other health care institutions.

But the film that is left behind can give some microbes a chance to develop resistance while it keeps working to kill susceptible germs. Some bacteria pump the chemical out. Others put their fatty acids together using an enzyme other than the one that triclosan targets.[38]

Some experts fear that antibacterial products could let resistant microbes crowd out the skin's normal flora. Those are the microbes that normally live on a healthy person's skin. Until they could grow back, resistant microbes would face less competition for space and food. That might give an advantage to resistant strains.

One worry is that such microbes might be disease-causing bacteria. Another fear is that the tricks that could help microbes survive antibacterial products could let them resist antibiotics too.[39]

Critics also say we do not need to wipe out all the germs around us. "Bacteria are our friends," says Stuart B. Levy at Tufts University. "They help us more than they harm us." Among other things, they help digest foods. They decompose dead material so their elements can return to the environment. They crowd out disease-causing bacteria.

"It's only when they get out of line that we need to treat them," concludes Levy. "Therefore, we should not try to sterilize our world."[40]

Another worry is the "hygiene hypothesis." Are our homes too clean, and does that increase disease? Rates of asthma and allergies are higher than they were decades ago, note critics of antibacterial products. Without a normal balance of microbes around, children's immune systems might not grow and function right.[41]

Meanwhile, critics say, overuse of antibacterial products could keep them from working where they are really needed— in hospitals and other places where people are vulnerable to infections. The less selective pressure there is for resistant bacteria to develop, the better the products can protect such patients.[42] Meanwhile, hospitals are using more alcohol-based wipes to control the spread of infections too.

Beyond this, critics of antibacterial products say they do little good anyway. "Basically, all the studies have shown that there doesn't appear to be a public health benefit from their use in healthy homes," says Levy.[43] Disease rates are not lower in homes that use antibacterial products, so critics say plain soap and water are just fine.

In contrast, makers of antibacterial products say they are safe. People have used antibacterial wash products for over thirty years. Manufacturers say there is no evidence linking the products' use to the rise of drug-resistant diseases.[44]

Critics overstate their worries, says the Soap and Detergent Association. For example, one study found *E. coli* could become

Many common products contain antibacterial agents. Scientists disagree on what effect such chemicals may have on drug-resistant diseases.

resistant to triclosan in the lab. Yet that did not happen with other types of bacteria.[45]

Plus, say product makers, the laboratory is not the same as the real world. Laboratories are controlled settings. In real life, bacteria face many challenges. It would not be enough to resist triclosan or other antibacterial agents. They would also have to survive everything else in the environment.

"The ecology that it needs to work in is very different," stresses George Fischler with The Dial Corporation.[46] Skin, in particular, has a very stable group of resident flora—microbes that live there almost all the time. In general, they are less susceptible to antibacterial products than other microbes. They also survive sunlight, cleaning chemicals, and most other things people do with their hands every day.

> One expert says, "Bacteria are our friends. They help us more than they harm us."

One study compared thirty homes that used antibacterial products to thirty homes that did not. The nonuser homes had more bacteria of the types being studied. Meanwhile, bacteria in the user homes were no less susceptible to antibiotics than those in the other homes.[47]

The hygiene hypothesis is "pretty much nonsense," adds Fischler. Microbes are all around us, and it is not really the job of antibacterial products to kill all germs anyway. "They don't sterilize the skin," explains Fischler. "They're there primarily to eliminate those transient organisms that get passed around."[48]

For example, people could pick up other microbes from contact with sick people, preparing food, changing diapers, or other activities. After all, not all homes are healthy homes. Plus, even if people are generally healthy, many want to keep these other types of microbes away. "If we can develop a product that reduces the risk of moving bacteria around, that's a good thing," says Fischler.[49]

Makers of antibacterial products feel they have a safe and appropriate use. Meanwhile, critics question whether it is worth taking even a hypothetical risk on the products adding to the problem of drug-resistant diseases. The debate goes on.

Out into the Environment

What happens when antibacterial products get washed down the drain? They go into a septic tank or through the sewers to wastewater treatment plants. The same thing happens with any antibiotic residues in people's urine or feces.

Wastewater plants break down wastes and decontaminate water before releasing it. But the basic process is not meant to destroy antimicrobial products that may be in the water. Thus, treatment plants can release residues into the environment.

Animals excrete antibiotic residues or breakdown products too. They can also wind up in lakes and rivers. Or they can get into soil when farmers use manure as fertilizer. Plant sprays with antibiotics can also get washed into soil or water by rain.[50]

Scientists at the U.S. Geological Survey tested water from 139 streams in thirty states. Over a dozen human and animal antibiotics showed up, as well as triclosan.[51] Could low levels of antibiotics in the environment exert some selective pressure for bacteria to develop antibiotic resistance? How might that affect human health?

In 2004, an international commission released a report on pollution in the Great Lakes. The report expressed the fear that farmers' use of antibiotics, plus drug-resistant bacteria in nature, "may present the greatest risk" to human health and the environment. As support, the authors relied on a 2002 study that noted that various waterborne pathogens have high risks of fatality. Thus, the potential for drug-resistant waterborne pathogens could become a major health threat.[52]

In another study, several catfish caught in Virginia's Pocomoke River had drug-resistant bacteria. Those bacteria matched strains found in locally grown chickens.[53] The bacteria probably came from the farms' use of antibiotics.

The Animal Health Institute and National Chicken Council said that the report was "just hype."[54] Nothing proved where the bacteria came from, they argued. Plus, nothing proved that they were making people sick.

Right now, there are no firm answers on what antimicrobial chemicals do in the environment. The questions themselves worry some scientists. Others take a wait-and-see approach and want to see more studies.

Special Problems

On a global scale, the problem of drug-resistant diseases is making it harder to fight three of the world's deadliest diseases: HIV/AIDS, tuberculosis, and malaria. Bioterrorism is a growing threat too. Just how does the dilemma of drug-resistant diseases factor into these special problems?

HIV and Its Impact

Up to 40 million people may be infected with human immunodeficiency virus, or HIV—the virus that causes AIDS. HIV is a type of virus called a retrovirus. It uses genetic material called RNA and a chemical called reverse transcriptase to take over cell functions. This genetic hijacking process makes the virus especially difficult to fight.

Body fluids from infected people transmit HIV. Those fluids include blood, semen, and other secretions. People who engage in unprotected sex outside a monogamous relationship are at high risk. (Monogamous here means permanent and with no other partners for either person.) People who use illegal drugs intravenously also have a high risk of getting HIV.

HIV targets certain white blood cells called CD4+ T cells, or T-helper cells. Normally, those cells coordinate the body's defense against infectious disease. Once HIV takes over, those cells stop doing their job. They become HIV virus factories instead.

For a while the body makes more CD4+ T cells. Over time, though, HIV invades more and more target cells. Eventually, HIV overwhelms the immune system.

As this book goes to press, there is no cure for HIV/AIDS. There is no vaccine yet either. Certain medicines called anti-retroviral drugs can control the spread of HIV inside the body. They can delay the onset of serious sickness and prolong people's quality of life for years. The earlier drug therapy starts, the more likely it is to help. That is why any people who have done things that put them at risk for HIV should get tested for the virus. Anyone entering a sexual relationship should first make certain his or her partner gets tested for HIV and other sexually transmitted diseases.

However, the HIV virus does not respond to the medicines forever. After repeated rounds of antiretroviral drugs, the virus can mutate enough to resist various medicines. Over half of HIV/AIDS patients may eventually fail to respond to antiretroviral drugs.[1]

Once the virus mutates, patients can pass on drug-resistant HIV to other people. In one study, over 12 percent of recently infected people had HIV strains that already resisted at least one drug.[2] Since they had not previously taken the medicines themselves, the patients obviously got the drug-resistant strains from someone else.

Early testing of HIV strains lets doctors tailor treatment to use whatever drugs may still work. Surveillance—collection of data about the disease—helps too. Then public health authorities know just what they are up against and how likely medications are to help, in general. The biggest fear, though, is that patients may be left without any medicines to control the virus. Then full-blown AIDS and death come much sooner.

Pharmaceutical companies and other researchers are trying to develop an effective HIV vaccine. Meanwhile, they are working on new drugs to help control the virus. Those drugs may be the best hope for people who get infected by HIV.

The problem of drug-resistant HIV is getting worse. Things are especially bad in developing countries. Many regions lack enough trained doctors. Without proper guidance, patients may not get the right medicines or take them properly. Plus, many drugs sold in those areas are cheap copycat versions of other medicines. Without quality medicines and adequate care, the percentage of drug-resistant strains could become even higher.

As those strains spread, the worldwide epidemic could get worse. On the other hand, no access to drugs would doom patients to die sooner.[3] The dilemma underscores the need to get quality medicines to developing countries at lower costs. If and when scientists develop a vaccine, it must get quickly to people in Africa and other countries where the AIDS epidemic is at its worst.

Even when drugs help delay full-blown AIDS, patients' immune systems eventually weaken. The patients become prey to opportunistic infections. Basically, the invading pathogens seize the "opportunity" to cause sickness.

Where other people's immune systems might readily fight such infections, an HIV patient does not have those defenses.

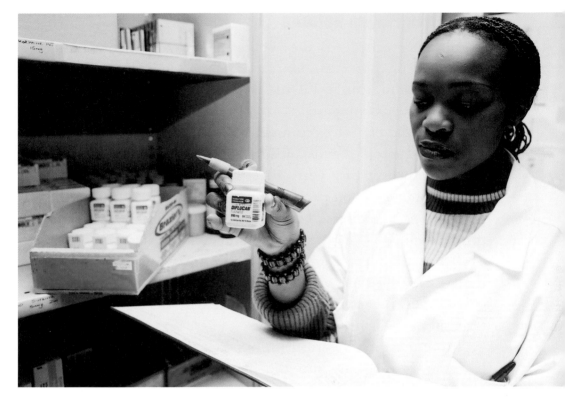

There is no cure for AIDS, but antiretroviral drugs can slow down its course. In addition, medications such as Diflucan can treat the opportunistic infections associated with AIDS. The drug's maker, Pfizer, donates large quantities of Diflucan to developing nations.

A bout of the flu or even the common cold can make an HIV patient extremely ill.

More serious pathogens invade too. Patterns of pneumonia cases initially clued medical researchers in to the existence of HIV/AIDS. Brain infections can result too.

Tuberculosis, or TB, especially wreaks havoc on patients with HIV/AIDS. The two diseases act like "gasoline and a match," says Lee Reichman at the National Tuberculosis Center.[4] Patients with HIV/AIDS are more likely to get TB. And when AIDS immobilizes the immune system, TB roams freely throughout the body.

The White Plague Returns

People once called TB the "white plague." In theory, just a single cell of *Mycobacterium tuberculosis* can trigger the TB. Because people catch TB by breathing in the bacteria, the disease is very contagious.

Under the best of circumstances, TB is tough to treat. The growth and spread of resistant strains make matters much worse. Even today, over fifty years after the debut of antibiotics, TB infects about 2 billion people—roughly one third of the world's population. The disease kills between 2 million and 3 million people each year—more than any other single infection.[5]

When TB infects someone, the immune system tries to fight it off. Cells called macrophages engulf them. But the hard, waxy coat of the TB bacterium is an effective defense. Often the bacteria survive. Then they multiply.

More macrophages rush in, but that does not stop the TB bacteria. They break into the macrophages, multiply inside them, and then burst out. If more macrophages attack, the bacteria take them over too.

The bacteria clump together, making it even harder for macrophages to attack. The clumps create small nodules, called tubercles. Bacteria in the tubercles multiply and send daughter cells into the bloodstream and lymphatic system.

Tuberculosis—once known as the "white plague"—currently infects about 2 billion people, or one third of the world's population.

If the immune system gets the upper hand again, it walls bacteria off into lumps of scar tissue. The infection becomes latent, or inactive—sometimes for decades. The person may not show symptoms, but a skin test can usually detect the bacteria's presence.

When someone's body can no longer control the infection, the walls around the tubercles break down. The disease becomes

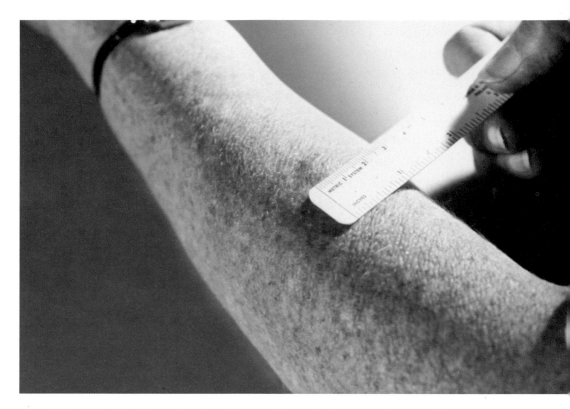

This patient is shown having her reaction site tested after receiving a TB test. In 1969, when this photo was taken, drug-resistant tuberculosis was not the serious problem it is today.

active again, and bacteria spread throughout the body. Each year, about 8 million people develop active TB.[6]

As patients begin showing symptoms, they become highly contagious. Pockets of phlegm and pus in the lungs lead to chronic coughing, which releases bacteria into the air. Patients have constant breathing problems. Fatigue, anemia, night sweats, and dull chest pain plague people with TB too. The disease spreads and infects the kidneys, digestive system, and bones. Consumption is another name for TB, and it aptly describes how the active disease eats away at a person.

As the twentieth century began, TB was the second leading cause of death in the United States, behind infections described as pneumonia and/or influenza.[7] Then in 1943, Selman Waksman and his team discovered streptomycin. The drug became the first antibiotic to treat TB. Patients could not just live longer. They could be cured.

But *Mycobacterium tuberculosis* is hardy, and resistance quickly became a problem. To fight drug-resistant TB, scientists searched for other antibiotics. Within the next two decades, they had a small arsenal of TB drugs. For example, researchers discovered para-aminosalicyclic acid (PAS) in 1946. By 1952, scientists had discovered isoniazid and pyrazinamide. The 1960s added ethambutol and rifampin.[8]

Using multiple drugs to fight TB became standard practice. If one drug did not kill the bacteria, another would do the job. Eventually, the number of TB cases dropped, and so did spending on programs to identify and control the disease in the United States. Unfortunately, complacency led to problems. By the late 1970s, TB rates were on the rise again in the United States.

One problem is that patients must take medicines for at least six to nine months. Otherwise, the bacteria have a chance to develop resistance. Patients can get sick again and spread the resistant strain to others. Drug-resistant strains have been a big factor in the jump in TB cases.

Starting in the 1980s, HIV infection caused TB rates to rise. Poverty and homelessness also played a big role. Patients often could not afford medicine. Plus, if they had no home, following up on treatment was much harder.

By the early 1990s, doctors were discovering more than four thousand new cases per year in the United States. The biggest concentration was in New York City.[9] When twelve inmates and a guard at New York state prisons died from drug-resistant TB in 1991, the news made the front page of *The New York Times*.[10] Public health experts worried about massive epidemics.

Public health authorities finally got America's minor epidemic under control, but it took a massive effort. New York

City spent about $100 million. Nationwide, excess public health expenditures to fight TB came to about $1 billion.[11]

Now, however, the same medicines that once worked routinely are no longer a sure thing. Doctors had faced antibiotic resistance before with TB, but they could usually count on the strongest drugs to work. Now even the full arsenal of TB drugs might not be enough to cure someone.

Generally, medical experts define multi-drug-resistant TB (MDR-TB) as cases that resist both isoniazid and rifampin— the two strongest TB drugs. Other drugs might still work. However, they often do not work as well, require prolonged treatment, or have more side effects. MDR-TB cases cost more too—up to $250,000 per case.[12]

Now, doctors in the United States and Canada usually test a patient's TB strain to see which drugs will work. Meanwhile, they start them on at least two antibiotics.[13] If testing shows resistance to a drug, doctors change the medicines. Ideally, they add at least two new drugs at a time. By doing so, they hope to give any resistant bacteria a one-two knockout punch. Yet even that cannot guarantee success over MDR-TB.

TB remains a problem in the United States and Canada. The disease is even more of a problem elsewhere. About three hundred thousand new cases of MDR-TB occur each year in the world, says WHO. About ninety thousand strains of the bacteria have some level of resistance.[14]

High TB rates add to countries' economic hardships, creating a spiraling problem. Beyond that, some societies stigmatize TB patients and their families. As a result, some people avoid treatment, get sicker, and spread the disease. Other people may seek treatment but find themselves out of a job or otherwise unable to earn money. No wonder the majority of all TB cases and TB deaths take place in the world's poorest countries.

When patients in developing countries can get medicines, they often do not follow through on orders for when, how, and how long to take each drug. Families may not have enough money for at least six months of treatment. Or the need to find paying jobs means people do not stay in one place long enough to complete treatment.

Unfortunately, skipping too many doses or stopping the medicines too soon leaves the door open for the bacteria that are less susceptible to thrive. Meanwhile, the patients can spread drug-resistant disease to people around them.

To deal with TB, WHO and other groups strongly recommend a method called DOTS, for "Direct Observed Treatment Short-course." With DOTS, trained personnel follow specific procedures for diagnosing TB. Then they administer medicines

HIV and drug-resistant TB are especially serious problems in developing countries. Here health care workers at a clinic discuss how to diagnose opportunistic infections in HIV patients and treat them with donated medicines.

on a set schedule and supervise their use. The goal is to make sure TB patients get all the medicines they need, when they need them. This is especially important in MDR-TB cases, which require the right mix of medicines and treatment for up to two years, versus six to nine months for other strains.[15]

DOTS also improves the chances that patients will comply with the treatment program. That reduces the chances that an initially susceptible strain will become resistant later. Better compliance also makes it less likely that patients will spread TB to others.

DOTS is not perfect, though. Providing the needed level of supervision is expensive. Plus, although DOTS works better than unsupervised treatment, the programs need a stable environment to work. Sadly, TB rates are high in some of the world's least politically stable areas.[16] As a separate matter, common testing methods call for patients to cough up enough phlegm. Many young children cannot do that. The test also misses many TB cases in people with HIV.

The problem of MDR-TB is especially bad in the former Soviet Union. In 2004, Paul Nunn of WHO's Stop TB program dubbed it "the MDR capital of the world."[17]

Even before the Soviet Union collapsed, resources for public health were paltry. Prisons were cramped and crowded too. Afterward, with the economy in shambles, crime rates rose. By 2002, over one million inmates were in Russia's jails.

Living in such close quarters, prisoners freely exchanged germs, including TB. Up to 10 percent of Russia's prison inmates have active, infectious TB. Over 80 percent have latent TB that could later become active. About three hundred thousand inmates leave each year, bringing the infection—including a high rate of MDR-TB—into the general population. When another three hundred thousand prisoners come in to replace them, they become exposed to the disease too.[18]

Russia's TB rates skyrocketed, even while the country had

low rates of HIV infection. Now increased intravenous drug use and higher rates of prostitution have pushed up HIV rates.[19] Given the link between HIV and TB, Russia's problem with MDR-TB will likely get worse.

As an added complication, many countries, including Russia and Eastern European countries, have used a TB vaccine called the BCG vaccine.[20] (The United States and the Netherlands never used it.) Developed in 1921, the vaccine helped young children somewhat. But it did little, if anything, to protect against TB once people got older.[21] Despite this, various countries still use the vaccine.

Not only did the vaccine not give long-term protection, but it also made it very hard to detect TB. People who had the BCG vaccine can test positive on a skin test for TB, whether they have the disease or not. The false positives make the test meaningless for them. Meanwhile, if they do have TB, they might spread it to others.[22] This causes problems in countries that used the vaccine heavily. It also makes it harder to screen people coming into the United States from other countries.

As this book goes to press, TB remains the leading infectious disease killer worldwide among persons over age five. Despite the medical advances of the twentieth century, TB is killing more people now than ever before.[23]

The Menace of Malaria

If you live in the United States and Canada, bug bites are annoying, but they are rarely deadly. In Africa and other parts of world, it is a different story. Get bitten by the wrong kind of insect, and you could get malaria or another fatal disease.

Anopheles mosquitoes transmit the *Plasmodium* parasites that cause malaria. Insecticide-spraying programs during the 1950s and 1960s got rid of most malaria-carrying mosquitoes in Latin America and Asia. Unfortunately, malaria is still a huge problem in Africa. In part, African countries could not adequately support irrigation and drainage projects that would go along with mass spraying so mosquitoes would not breed. Also, disease-carrying mosquitoes are so plentiful that the problem seemed too enormous.[24]

For a long time, the drug chloroquine worked like a charm. Then people took it for all sorts of fevers, not just malaria. Over time, the parasites developed resistance. Sulfadoxine-pyrimethamine, or SP, became doctors' next choice. The parasites became resistant to that too.[25]

In Africa alone, malaria kills over one million people each year. Other victims are too sick to work. Some poor families spend a third of their yearly incomes trying to treat the disease.

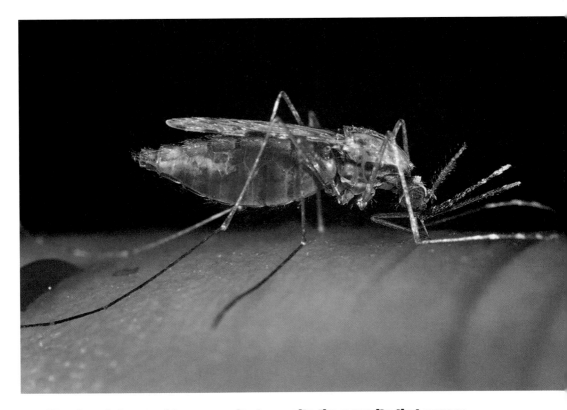

The _Anopheles gambiae_ mosquito transmits the parasite that causes malaria. Treatment with the drug chloroquine no longer effectively controls the disease.

That keeps people locked in poverty. Meanwhile, it hinders economic growth in areas that sorely need it. Costs of lost output run around $12 billion a year.[26]

Artemisinin-based combination therapies (ACTs) show great promise. ACTs use several medicines, including a fast-acting drug derived from the sweet wormwood plant. Treating the disease with several medicines also cuts the risk of developing resistance. ACTs work especially well for travelers who get malaria while visiting abroad.

Unfortunately, many parts of Africa and other developing countries lack clinics. Plus, at two dollars per dose, ACTs cost far more than most Africans can afford. So, patients continue to take the older, often ineffective medicines for about ten cents a pill. That seems better than nothing.[27]

Making ACTs accessible to people who need them is critical to controlling drug-resistant malaria. Prevention strategies are key too. Better use of insecticides, netting, and other steps can cut infection rates dramatically. Sadly, many people cannot afford them either.

Improved treatment and prevention strategies will not eliminate malaria. Yet they could save millions of people over the course of a decade. Perhaps the biggest challenges are political and economic. Will the international community help provide resources to fight the menace of drug-resistant malaria?

The Threat of Bioterrorism

Disease is devastating enough when it happens naturally. When people deliberately release pathogens on others, it is terrifying. Even before the 2001 anthrax attacks in the United States, experts were gearing up to deal with the prospect of bioterrorism.

A wake-up call came in 1995, when a teenage boy in Madagascar became sick with drug-resistant plague. *Yersinia pestis* caused the teen's illness. Fleas on rodents carry the disease and can transmit it to humans who come into contact with them. Three antibiotics failed to cure the teen. Fortunately, another drug finally worked, and the boy lived.[28]

The boy's case occurred naturally. Yet it is the kind of disease that causes concern among public health experts who worry about bioterrorism. If the drug-resistant plague became widespread, it could have killed thousands. Before the Soviet Union collapsed in 1991, researchers there may have worked on such a biological weapon.[29] The CDC notes that terrorists might still potentially use plague as a biological weapon.[30]

Plague is not the only potential pathogen in bioterrorists' arsenals. Anthrax, tularemia, botulism, and viral fevers rank high on the priority list for public health officials.

Smallpox is a big worry too. Worldwide vaccination programs

Plague can be spread by fleas on rodents. Here a man sets rat traps as part of a plague study.

officially wiped out the disease in 1977. Afterward, routine vaccinations ended, so most people now do not have vaccine protection against the disease. However, some smallpox samples stayed in labs for study. If terrorists got hold of those samples and released smallpox in the general population, the disease could be highly fatal. Thus, smallpox also ranks high on CDC's priority list for fighting bioterrorism.[31]

If a bioterrorist threat occurs again, public fear may worsen the problem of drug resistance. After the 2001 anthrax scare, Cipro prescriptions and sales skyrocketed as people rushed to get the drug. Even if they had not been exposed, many wanted the drug on hand, just in case. While some doctors resisted giving unnecessary prescriptions, others went along to satisfy worried patients.[32]

Such stockpiling reduces drug supplies for patients who really need them. When people take the drugs unnecessarily, that also increases the odds that drug-resistant infections can strike later on. Both effects limit the ability of medicines to fight bioterrorism and other public health threats.

Seeking Solutions

Scientists are working on different approaches to the dilemma of drug-resistant diseases. But finding workable solutions is a complex process.

Wanted: More Antibiotics

So far, the main answer to drug-resistant disease has been more drugs. Bacteria showed resistance to penicillin. To get around that, scientists changed its chemical structure. They made amoxycillin, methicillin, and other antibiotics. If bacteria could resist those medicines, doctors tried other antibiotics.

New antibiotics did not solve the problem of drug-resistant

disease. It was only a matter of time until bacteria would resist the newer drugs. Indeed, the more people used the newer drugs, the sooner resistance would show up.

Now the arsenal of medicines is running low. Even "last-resort" medicines like vancomycin face some drug-resistant bacteria.

"We need new drugs, because resistance has gotten out of hand," notes Stuart B. Levy at the Alliance for the Prudent Use of Antibiotics.[1] However, most large drug companies no longer do research and development (R&D) on new antibiotics. Money is a big reason.

The average cost of developing a drug and bringing it to market ranges from $450 million to $900 million.[2] To invest that kind of money in R&D, companies need a profit incentive. They want to get the biggest return from their R&D dollars.

Drug-resistant diseases are a problem, but many antibiotics still work well. For example, some pneumococcal bacteria resist amoxycillin. Yet that medicine is still often the drug of first choice. It usually has few side effects. Plus, it costs less than some other medicines.[3]

Even with resistant infections, doctors can usually try other drugs. Indeed, hundreds of antibacterial drugs are on the market.[4] Thus, the market for new antibiotics is smaller than it was in the past. Companies question whether they would get a good return on their investment.

Indeed, some health professionals might use newer antibiotics as "last-resort" drugs. That would further limit their sales. Beyond that, antibiotics generally are just not as profitable as some other types of medicines.

"What's pretty clear is that drug companies don't make as much money off antibiotics—individually, per antibiotic—as they do from other drug products," says John Powers at the FDA. "The reason for that is that most antibiotics are taken for a short period of time."[5]

Antibiotic treatments usually last fourteen days or less. Sometimes they take just one or a few days. Few diseases require several months of antibiotics. That naturally limits potential sales—and profits.

In contrast, chronic diseases need long-term care, and drugs to treat those diseases can have huge sales. Asthma patients take medicines for years. Patients with high blood pressure must control it for the rest of their lives. The same goes for diabetes patients and their blood sugar levels.

Various psychiatric diseases also require long-term use of medicines. For example, patients typically take drugs for anxiety or depression for years.

In light of this, antibiotics are not the most profitable option for big drug companies. In 2003, Pfizer's Zithromax was America's best-selling antibiotic, with sales of $2 billion. The same year, though, Pfizer's cholesterol-control drug Lipitor brought in $9 billion.[6]

Regulatory hurdles, including attorney fees, add to the cost of getting a drug to market. In the United States, the FDA has the job of making sure medicines are both safe and effective. Companies need FDA approval at multiple steps. The reason for each hurdle is to protect American consumers.

Preclinical testing is the first step after a company develops a drug. Animal studies help researchers see how the drug works. The studies flag safety issues too. The FDA reviews the company's materials and decides if it is safe to study the drug in humans.

Clinical research comes next. Phase I studies look at a drug's effects in healthy volunteers. How does the body process the drug? What response does the drug cause?

Phase II studies focus on sick people that the drug could treat. Experiments compare the new drug with either a placebo, such as a sugar pill, or an existing medicine. Results tell whether a drug works. They also give clues about short-term safety and possible side effects.

Phase III clinical trials can involve thousands of patients. They are much more involved than Phase II studies. They also can involve patients with multiple illnesses who take various medicines.

Along the way, companies sometimes get approval to use experimental drugs for compassionate use cases. Patients who are very ill and for whom no other medicines have worked try the drug. Their data goes into the files too.

Because of the cost of bringing new drugs to market, most large pharmaceutical companies do not do research and development on new antibiotics.

After the Phase III trials, companies submit detailed reports to the FDA. Submissions run to thousands or even a million pages. The agency reviews the data. It may hold meetings for public comments too.

The FDA approves a drug company's application if it finds that the medicine is safe and effective for its intended use. Among other things, the agency looks at risks and benefits. Higher risks of toxicity may be acceptable if a drug is used to treat a lethal disease. They might also be worthwhile if nothing else can help a serious condition. But people would not want such risks if a disease was not serious, or if there were safer medicines. Even after the FDA approves a drug, it may ask for more studies.[7]

In many cases, companies sell medicines in other countries too. Thus, they often prepare submittals for the European Union or other governments at the same time they seek FDA approval. The whole process of getting government approvals costs a lot and can take years. There is no guarantee of success, either.

Take a look at Tygacil. Researchers developed the injectable drug in 1992 as "exactly the kind of drug we need for resistant infection," says Steven Projan at maker Wyeth Pharmaceuticals.[8]

A research chemist at a pharmaceutical company conducts an experiment. There are many steps in the process of bringing a drug to market.

However, the FDA did not approve the drug until 2005—more than a dozen years later.

"This drug might become the poster child for how long it takes to develop something that's clinically useful," said Projan in 2004.[9] Tygacil's clinical trials included patients in nearly seven hundred hospitals in thirty-five countries. Each patient's data would fill a thick binder. Submissions for the FDA and the European Union ran to millions of pages. Preparing all the data demanded by the agencies took years and cost millions of dollars.

Even if Tygacil becomes a therapeutic success, it may not be a commercial success. Some doctors may use it only for last-resort cases. Plus, the drug's patent will expire in 2013. After drug patents expire, other companies can make and sell their own versions. Consumers typically pay less for such generic versions than they do for brand-name prescription drugs. But then the generic manufacturers do not have to pay the initial patent holders anything toward research and development costs.

FDA officials defend their role and their close scrutiny of new drugs. Antibiotics have one of the best track records for approval and review time at the agency.[10] Thus, the FDA is reluctant to relax its requirements. After all, if a drug company cannot satisfy the agency that any new medicine is safe and effective, why should it go on the market?

Aside from the regulatory hurdles, developing new medicines involves big business risks. A promising idea might not work in the lab. Or a drug may work in the lab, but do poorly in clinical trials. This all adds to the average costs for bringing new drugs to market.

"Most of what we do does not result in new drugs," admits Steven Projan at Wyeth. Researchers persist, he says, because they want to save lives. Yet the bottom line still matters: "Unless what we do returns something on the investment, then we're not going to be able to do anything. . . . And if we invest in things that have no return on investment, that actually cost us money, then we're not going to be around to find any cures for any diseases."[11]

Meanwhile, having just a few large companies working on new antibiotics is not enough.[12] Government subsidies for R&D are one possibility. Special programs already exist to fund "orphan drugs"—medicines to help fewer than two hundred thousand patients in the United States. Even then, medicines for chronic conditions would have a bigger market than new antibiotics. Plus, many people might object if tax money helped large pharmaceutical companies earn more profits.

Meanwhile, some smaller firms are getting into the field. In late 2003, the FDA approved daptomycin for treating certain skin infections. Cubist Pharmaceuticals in Massachusetts, which sells the drug as Cubicin, was founded in 1992. Another relative new-comer to the antibiotics field is SIGA Technologies in New York and Oregon, which was founded in 1995. Rib-X Pharmaceuticals in Connecticut entered the antibiotics field in 2001.

After all, worldwide antibiotics sales are nearly $30 billion.[13] That is still a big enough market to interest able researchers and investors.

Vaccines, Peptides, and Plants

Antibiotics are not the only way to fight bacterial diseases. Vaccines prevent people from getting a disease in the first case. If people do not get sick, drug resistance is much less of an issue.

In 2000, the U.S. government approved the vaccine Prevnar. While more than sixty types of pneumococcal bacteria exist, the vaccine targets the seven types most likely to make children sick. Those seven also cause the most drug-resistant disease cases. Now when a child gets a pneumococcal infection, antibi-otics are more likely to work.

Within three years, drug-resistant pneumococcal infections among young children dropped. Penicillin-resistant infections fell

88 percent among children under two, while rates for children from two to four years old fell 71 percent.[14] Resistance rates also dropped among older groups, who might otherwise have caught the disease from young family members.[15]

Nabi Biopharmaceuticals in Florida has come up with a staph vaccine. Called StaphVAX, it helps the body's immune system identify invading bacteria as germs. The body can then fight off infection with its own antibodies. As this book goes to press, the company is doing Phase III clinical trials with kidney patients, who pick up infections very easily. The next step would be FDA approval.[16] In 2004, Nabi also got a patent for vaccines against *Enterococci*, another type of bacteria that is a problem in hospitals.[17]

Vaccines can help, but they will not get rid of all drug-resistant diseases. Even with a good TB vaccine, for example, the number of TB cases would drop by only about one third.[18] Too many people already carry the disease. TB would stick around even after thirty years. Public health authorities would still need to track patients and follow up on treatment to rein in rates of drug-resistant TB.

Another approach might use chemicals in the immune system. IVIG, or intravenous immunogammaglobulin, has antibodies collected from many people's blood plasma and treated to make it safe. Generally, doctors use IVIG to treat immune system disorders. But some studies show it can also help treat aggressive staph and strep infections, especially those that cause toxic shock syndrome—a sudden-onset disease in which multiple organs fail and the body goes into severe shock. IVIG might have potential to treat drug-resistant strains of the bacteria too.[19]

Peptides are another possible weapon. These short amino acid chains are on people's eyes, skin, tongue, and other surfaces. As part of the body's first line of defense against disease, peptides break apart some harmful bacteria. Understanding

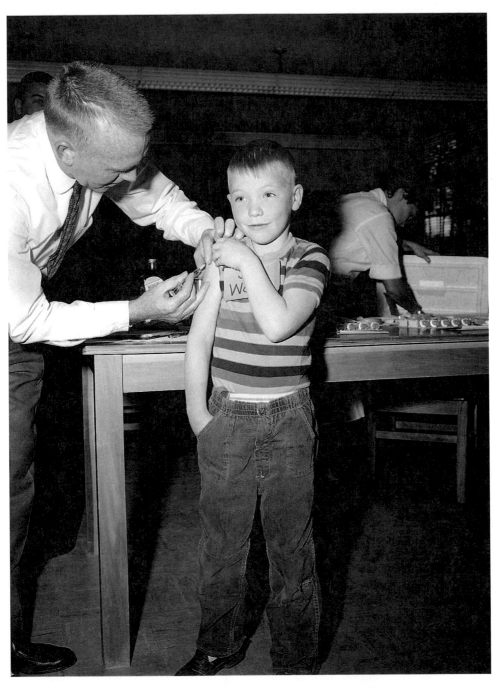

A boy receives a shot for measles as part of a vaccination campaign in 1962. If vaccines prevent people from getting sick in the first place, antibiotic resistance becomes less of a problem.

how peptides work could help scientists engineer new drugs to destroy microbes.[20]

Researchers are looking at animal peptides too. Alligators almost never get sick. And while Indonesia's Komodo dragons have highly toxic bacteria in their mouths, the reptiles themselves do not get sick. Such animal peptides could one day help develop new medicines.[21]

Plants might help too. For example, the barberry bush not only makes its own antibiotic, but it also makes a substance to stop bacteria from pumping the chemical out of their cells. The combination of chemicals killed staph in lab experiments.[22]

Garlic and St. John's wort may have useful antibacterial properties too, and they are already available at health food stores.[23] At this time, however, the FDA does not regulate food supplements, and these herbs' medical uses are still subject to further study.

Beating Bacteria at Their Own Game

Most of the bacteria in and around us are harmless. Many are even helpful. Why not crowd out bad microbes with good ones? This is the concept behind probiotics.

For example, yogurt has live *acidophilus* cultures. Eating it may help people keep a good balance of flora. That might cut down on intestinal and vaginal infections.[24]

ConjuGon Inc. in Wisconsin has another idea. Remember that bacteria sometimes swap genes with each other. Why not get harmless bacteria to sneak genes into bad bacteria? The genes could then disarm the disease-causing traits in the bad bacteria. The company has gotten a patent and raised some money for further studies.[25]

Other research tries to mess up bacteria's signals. Bacteria have no brains. Yet somehow cells signal each other to form colonies and biofilms. If scientists could disrupt those signals, bacteria might not be able to make someone sick.[26]

A Different Kind of Germ Warfare

If bacteria are going to make people sick, why not make the bacteria sick? That is the idea behind bacteriophage therapy. Bacteriophages, or phages for short, are viruses that attack bacteria.

"Germs have their own germs," says Elizabeth Kutter at Evergreen State College.[27] Almost anywhere bacteria live, phages are probably there too—whether that is near hot vents in the oceans, animals' guts, or even in wastewater treatment sludge.

French-Canadian Felix d'Herelle and Englishman Edward Twort independently discovered bacteriophages nearly one hundred years ago. Temperate phages integrate their DNA into bacteria and let the bacteria keep functioning more or less normally. Scientists use temperate phages for things like genetic engineering, when they want to make bacteria into factories to produce a desired substance, such as a gene or hormone. Temperate phages can be dangerous too. For example, people get diphtheria—a respiratory illness—when a bacteriophage gene causes *Corynebacterium diptheriae* to release a toxin.[28]

In contrast, virulent phages get into bacteria cells, reproduce themselves, and soon burst out—killing the host cells. These killer phages show the greatest promise for treating disease.

Phage therapy research thrived during the early twentieth century. Then antibiotics came on the scene, and most North Americans lost interest in phages. Meanwhile, researchers in the Soviet Union pursued the topic.

In 1923, George Eliava and d'Herelle started the Eliava Institute in what today is the Republic of Georgia. The institute found phages to treat many diseases, and phage therapy became a standard medical tool in the region. Phage production peaked in the 1970s and 1980s. It then fell drastically after the Soviet Union collapsed.

Despite funding cutbacks, the Eliava Institute still treats

Researchers find bacteriophages in a wide range of places. Before sewage water gets disinfected, it probably holds a variety of phages.

patients with phage therapy. With drug-resistant disease on the rise, researchers around the world are taking note. Patients are finding new hope too.

Canadian doctors told Alfred Gertler his foot had to be amputated. Gertler, a diabetic, had a foot infection that resisted every antibiotic they tried. Desperate for a cure, Gertler traveled thousands of miles to the Republic of Georgia. Ten months after staying at the Eliava Institute, his foot and ankle were healed.[29]

Phages may have a big advantage in such external applications, says Kutter. Diabetics' poor circulation makes it hard for intravenous antibiotics to get where they are needed.

Antibiotics put on the skin have little effect deep down. Either way, there would be too little of the antibiotic. That often selects for resistant bacteria.

In contrast, phages applied to the skin get more potent as they go deep down. On the skin's surface, the phages infect the first cells they find and multiply there. Those cells release more phages that then go deeper and infect more bacteria.

"You have this exponentially growing number," says Kutter.[30] Once the phages subdue the infection, their numbers drop off. After that, the immune system's white blood cells clear them out of the body.

Kutter and her team at Evergreen State College in Washington are doing ongoing research into phage therapy. They often cooperate with scientists and students from the Eliava Institute. One promising project aims to get a very dangerous strain of *Escherichia coli*, known as *E. coli* O157:H7, out of meat. The bacteria do not make food animals sick, but a few of them can make people deathly ill.

Rockefeller University in New York is doing phage research too. Private companies are also entering the field. Examples are PhageTech and Biophage Pharma in Quebec, Exponential Biotherapies in New York, and Intralytix in Maryland.[31] Some projects explore how phages might treat human infections directly. Others study how phages attack bacteria to find new targets for drugs. Other projects look at possible applications for plants and animals.

Phage therapy has its drawbacks, however. Phages abound in sewage, soil, and other bacteria-rich places. Yet finding the right one to treat a disease can be tricky.

"They're quite specific," says Kutter. Many phages hit only some members of certain groups of bacteria. On the plus side, phages generally will not kill off most of the good bacteria in the body. Plus, says Kutter, there are about 10^{32} phages in

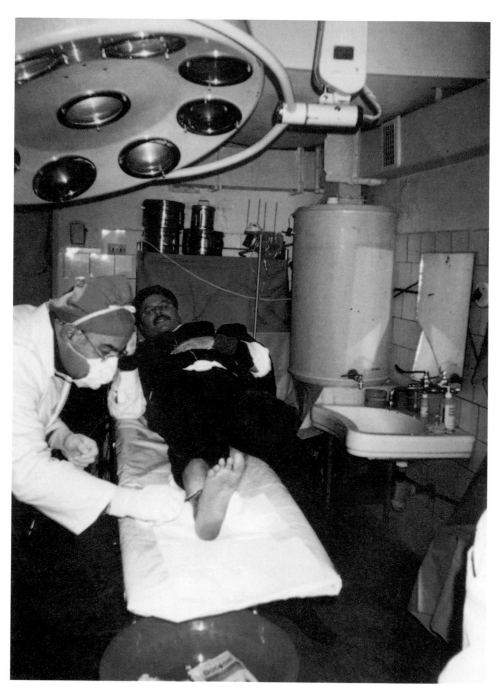

Alfred Gertler received phage therapy in the Republic of Georgia, saving his foot. With the rise in antibiotic resistance, new attention is being given to the potential of phages in treating disease.

nature (1, followed by 32 zeroes). Thus, chances are good that some phage somewhere could kill invading bacteria.[32]

Also, there are few "broad-spectrum" phages. Some illnesses, like Gertler's foot infection, even need "phage cocktails"— combinations of phages to attack bacteria.

The wide variety of phages raises regulatory questions too. Under the present model, the FDA would probably require approval for each phage or cocktail. Each set of clinical trials and submissions could cost millions of dollars.

Over time, bacteria can develop resistance to phages, just as they do to antibiotics. Phage researchers feel this is not a huge problem. In theory, the phages should also evolve to stay effective against the bacteria. But any time delays could spell problems for patients. And if the phage has changed, it might require another round of regulatory approval.

The specificity of phage therapy also means that most products would have a limited market. Indeed, many phages have been used for so long outside the United States that they probably could not get a patent. Both factors would limit potential profits.

Even if very few phages are used in therapy in the United States, they can still help battle bacteria. Genetic studies can identify proteins that phages use to attack bacteria's weak spots. In one study, for example, researchers studied twenty-six phages and found thirty-one previously unknown compounds.[33] Those compounds might lead to new drugs.

No approach offers an automatic cure-all for the dilemma of drug-resistant diseases. The more ideas scientists pursue, the better we can battle disease and find cures.

Time for Decisions

Drug-resistant diseases threaten to set back decades of medical advances. Fortunately, the problem is nowhere near the panic level—yet. Most antibiotics and other medicines still do their job most of the time.

Yet drug-resistant disease is by no means rare, either. To keep the problem from becoming a crisis, government, private companies, and researchers need to take action. Your decisions can make a difference too.

Beyond Borders

Does it seem as if drug-resistant malaria, TB, or other diseases affect only people in faraway lands? Guess again. Each day, millions of people travel internationally. Where airlines had only 2 million international passengers in 1950, the number was well over a billion per year as this century began.[1]

With so much travel, infectious disease can spread quickly around the globe. Just look at SARS—sudden acute respiratory syndrome. Scientists discovered the viral disease in 2003. Within months, it hopped around the globe from China to nearly a dozen other countries. SARS cases showed up in Canada and the United States.[2]

Drug-resistant gonorrhea showed up in Hawaii, Asia, and the Pacific Islands around 2000. By 2003, resistant strains of the sexually transmitted disease showed up in New York, Massachusetts, Indiana, and elsewhere too. By 2004, the rates of antibiotic resistance were high enough that the CDC changed its treatment recommendations.[3]

Strains of *Streptococcus pneumoniae* can now effectively survive various antibiotics. In some countries, rates of resistance against penicillin, macrolides, and tetracyclines are 30 percent or higher. Resistance against fluoroquinolone antibiotics is rising too. Cases are showing up in such far-flung places as Hong Kong, Canada, Ireland, and Spain.[4]

Screening travelers for disease is not always feasible, and legal concerns enter in too. Tests may take too much time. Results are not always reliable either, as experience with people who got the BCG vaccine shows.

Other countries' regulatory regimes have an effect too. Many medicines that are prescription only in the United States are over-the-counter (OTC) drugs in various other countries. Some of those countries have high rates of poverty and infectious disease. OTC status means that people in those countries can get antibiotics and other drugs more easily. But they can misuse the medicines more readily too. When they take the wrong medicine or wrong doses, they unwittingly select for drug-resistant microbes.

"Pirate" drugs are a problem in other countries too. Those cheap, unlicensed versions of drugs are often watered-down or less effective versions of medicines that were initially made by large drug companies. Instead of delivering a knockout punch to infectious disease, they can select for resistance.

With more than a billion international travelers flying every year, infectious diseases can spread quickly around the world.

Better and cheaper access to quality medicines is one answer to the pirate drug problem. Yet that may be easier said than done. Drug companies want a fair return on their R&D dollars. Defining what is fair is itself a huge debate. Private or public subsidies could help, but the funds would have to come from somewhere.

Of course, programs to improve medical services could go a long way toward cutting rates of drug-resistant disease. Raising the standard of living in developing countries could make a huge dent in resistant disease rates too. Poverty is one of the biggest risk factors for disease, especially with diseases like TB.

Meanwhile, time may be running out. As David Heymann of WHO's Communicable Diseases program explained:

> The world may only have a decade or two to make optimal use of many of the medicines presently available to stop infectious diseases. We are literally in a race against time to bring levels of infectious disease down worldwide, before the diseases wear the drugs down first.[5]

Scientific developments will not solve problems if they are not available to large sectors of the world's population. Developing countries need help to battle drug-resistant diseases. WHO can help, but its resources are limited. The organization and various experts look to the industrialized world—especially the United States—for assistance.

Yet foreign-aid decisions are not simple. International relations and political issues enter in. Government authorities may weigh aid decisions based on whether another country's interests mesh with their own aims. Corruption in foreign governments can also raise concerns about whether aid will get to people.

Plus, money to fight drug-resistant diseases on a global scale has to come from somewhere. A choice to spend money for one foreign-aid program could come at the cost of another worthwhile program. It could divert money from defense or domestic programs. Or it could come from higher taxes. Each choice could pit policy makers and segments of the public against each other.

Yet drug-resistant disease remains an international public health issue. And disease can spread anywhere. Compassion is one reason industrialized nations may help fight disease in developing countries. Self-interest is a strong motivation too.

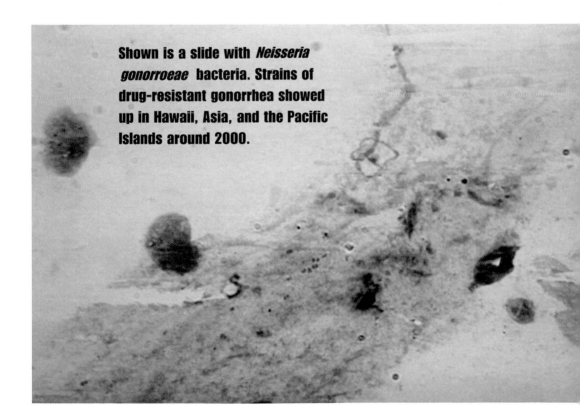

Shown is a slide with *Neisseria gonorroeae* bacteria. Strains of drug-resistant gonorrhea showed up in Hawaii, Asia, and the Pacific Islands around 2000.

Investing in Health

Scientists are following multiple paths to fight drug-resistant disease. But the fight requires resources. Research and development of treatments cost money.

If private companies will profit from such treatments, then it seems fair to expect investors to pay for R&D. Yet private companies claim the costs are too high, or that returns would be too low, compared to other options. Should government subsidize such efforts?

One 2003 Senate bill proposed incentives for companies to develop new antibiotics, antivirals, and other drugs.[6] Among other things, the bill would have allowed tax breaks, sped up regulatory approval, enhanced patent protection, and set up a fund to buy various drugs. The bill's goal was to thwart bioterrorism. But new medicines could also fight drug-resistant diseases.

Proposals to have government get involved raise various questions. One main issue is what strings, if any, should go along with any incentives to develop new drugs. Other issues involve the rights to any profits. And, as with many political matters, the issue of who would foot the bill is a huge question. Another sensitive issue is whether taxpayer money should subsidize drug companies' work. These questions have no easy answers.

Counting the Costs

Of course, the problem of drug-resistant diseases already carries high costs. Estimates range from around $7 billion per year all the way up to $30 billion. This would include bills for doctors, hospitals, lab tests, and drugs. It would also include increased insurance costs and expenses for medical facilities. Beyond that, there are costs for lost time from work, lost economic productivity, and so on. And these estimates are just for the United States.[7]

Drug-resistant diseases often last longer and are more severe than those that respond well to drug treatment. Given a choice, no individual would want to incur those costs. Perhaps the biggest fear is getting a disease that resists even last-resort treatments. If no medicines are available to treat disease, then the cost could be life itself.

Vancomycin-resistant staph and *Enterococci* infections are examples. Even when alternative treatments exist, they have no guarantee of success. Plus, medicines can be very expensive. As of 2002, the antibiotic Zyvox cost about $140 per day, while Synercid ran between $180 and $250 per day. Vancomycin, the older drug of last resort, cost only $14 per day, but giving someone the drug still usually entailed a hospital stay.[8]

Obviously, the less costly it is to treat infectious disease, the better. But lower cost alternatives will not be practical if resistance becomes too widespread.

What Are the Limits?

How far can government go in preventing or controlling outbreaks of disease? To some extent, it depends on who and where you are.

For example, schools can require students to get certain vaccinations. They can also send sick children home. This protects not just individual children, but also the school community.

Prisons have procedures for dealing with inmates who have various diseases. What if inmates object to tests or treatment? Federal court cases have said inmates can refuse a TB test if it goes against their religious beliefs. For example, people in the Rastafarian faith view the body as a Holy Temple of Jah-God. They believe any artificial chemical injections or drugs would defile or contaminate that temple. Even then, prisons can take steps to make sure inmates will not contaminate other people, such as requiring X-rays.[9] If someone refused even that, facilities might resort to isolation.

Quarantines of citizens who have done nothing wrong pose even trickier problems. A country that prides itself on freedom does not want to restrain citizens unless absolutely necessary. Yet contagious diseases like TB can threaten other people and spread drug-resistant strains.

In an emergency, public health authorities could use quarantine authority. In one case, for example, a court let New York health officials confine an HIV-positive woman with TB in a hospital while she underwent treatment. The woman had no stable address and had apparently been a prostitute too.[10]

Nevertheless, quarantine is a drastic remedy, since it restricts people's personal freedom. Concerns about constitutional rights also mean the government must follow procedures to protect individuals' due process rights. Thus, public health authorities hope they do not have to use that authority often.[11]

Personal Choices

What you do makes a difference too. Learning about drug-resistant diseases is a good start. Knowledge makes you an informed consumer of health care services.

Knowledge empowers you to develop informed opinions too. Review the evidence on different sides of issues relating to drug-resistant diseases. Take a stand on matters you feel strongly about.

Take a good look at your personal habits too. "One of the most important ways people can avoid getting a resistant infection is to avoid getting an infection altogether," stresses Richard Besser at the CDC. Toward that end, "Hand washing is really important."[12]

Wash before and after eating, before preparing food, and after using the bathroom. Scrub thoroughly for at least twenty seconds. In most cases, regular soap and water should work just fine.

Use common sense to reduce your risks of getting foodborne diseases. Wash fruits and vegetables before eating them. Be sure meat, fish, and eggs are fully cooked. Avoid contaminating cooked foods with utensils or dishes that have touched raw meats.

Watch out for food spoilage. Refrigerate cooked foods and dishes with mayonnaise promptly. Throw out any foods that are past their use dates.

Take care of your general health. Get enough sleep each night. Schedule regular exercise into your day, and eat a healthy diet.

Get regular checkups. Make sure you have all your vaccinations too. When you are in good shape, your immune system can do a better job of fighting off infections.

If you get a scrape or wound, wash it thoroughly. Apply an antiseptic and dressing to prevent infection. See your doctor right away if a wound does get infected.

If you get ill, do not spread your germs around. Stay home from school if you have a fever. Cover your mouth when you cough.

When you are sick, do not automatically ask your doctor for antibiotics. Many infections are viral. Antibiotics do nothing against them.

Do ask your doctor what steps can help you feel better sooner. Many doctors now provide handouts on how to deal with viral infections. For example, some medicines may help you breathe easier, control coughing, or relieve pain. Rest and extra fluids help too. Know when to check back with your doctor for any follow-up or if you still feel sick.

If your doctor does prescribe an antibiotic, ask why you need it. Then be sure to take all doses as directed. Even if you feel better quickly, *finish the prescription*. You do not want to let less susceptible bacteria fight back.

Read the fact sheets that come with prescription medicines too. These papers give important information about doses, possible side effects, and so on. Your pharmacist will gladly answer any questions you have.

Drug-resistant disease is a public health issue that affects your community, the country, and the world. Yet drug-resistant microbes attack people on the individual level. Your personal

Thorough hand washing can help prevent a wide range of infections—both viral and bacterial.

choices can help you stay healthy, while slowing the spread of drug-resistant diseases.

You cannot make yourself immune to every infection. But you can arm yourself with knowledge and become a savvy health care consumer. That is a good first step in dealing with any public health issue.

Chronology

1674—Antonie van Leeuwenhoek sees microbes with a homemade microscope.

1864—Louis Pasteur persuades French Academy of Sciences to accept the "germ theory" of disease.

1881—Robert Koch grows bacteria cultures for study.

1888—Edouard de Freudenreich discovers the antibiotic pyocyanase, but the drug is toxic and unstable.

1912—Salvarsan, developed by German scientist Paul Ehrlich, comes on the market to treat syphilis.

1915, 1917—Frederick Twort and Felix d'Herelle independently discover bacteriophages.

1929—Scottish scientist Alexander Fleming publishes his 1928 discovery of penicillin.

1939—René Dubos isolates the soil bacterium *Bacillus brevis,* which leads to the antibiotic gramicidin.

1942—Penicillin makes headlines for successfully treating hundreds of burn victims after the Cocoanut Grove fire in Boston.

1944—Selman Waksman, Albert Schatz, and Elizabeth Bugie discover streptomycin.

1945—The Nobel Prize in Medicine or Physiology goes to Alexander Fleming, Howard Florey, and Ernst Chain for their work on penicillin. Fleming warns of the potential for bacteria to become resistant to penicillin. Resistance shows up just one year later.

1946—Joshua Lederberg and Edward L. Tatum describe how bacteria can transfer genes to other cells by conjugation.

1947—The broad-spectrum antibiotic chloramphenicol is discovered.

1948—Tetracycline, a low-toxicity broad-spectrum antibiotic, goes on the market.

1951—FDA approves first antibiotic growth promoter for animals.

1956—Discovery of vancomycin.

1959—Multiple-drug-resistant *Shigella* and multiple-drug resistant *E. coli* appear; resistance to high-level streptomycin appears; methicillin is developed.

1961—First cases of methicillin-resistant *Staphylococcus aureus* (MRSA) show up.

1970—The National Nosocomial Infections Surveillance System begins collecting data on hospital-acquired infections.

1981—First AIDS cases appear in the United States.

1986—Sweden bans antibiotic growth promoters in farming.

1987—First vancomycin-resistant *Enterococci* cases appear.

1991—Drug-resistant TB cases make headlines in New York.

1995–1999—More European Union countries ban various antibiotic growth promoters.

1997—Japanese researchers find a strain of *Staphylococcus aureus* that resists all known antibiotics.

1999—The FDA approves Synercid (quinupristan-dalfopristin) and Zyvox (linolezid).

2001—First cases of Zyvox-resistant *Staphylococcus* and *Enterococcus*.

2003—McDonald's announces new global policy on antibiotics for its meat suppliers.

2004—The FDA approves Ketek (telithromycin).

2005—The FDA approves the broad-spectrum antibiotic Tygacil (tigecycline).

Chapter Notes

Chapter 1 Superbugs Attack

1. Jeff Passan, "Staph Lurks Silently as Sports Hazard," *Fresno Bee*, September 18, 2003, p. D1; Charles Ornstein and Gary Klein, "Outbreak of Staph Hits USC Team," *Los Angeles Times*, September 13, 2003, p. B1. See also "Official Brandon Hancock Web Page," February 6, 2004, <http://www-scf.usc.edu/~bhancock> (December 28, 2004).

2. Annysa Johnson, "Football Player Hospitalized in Suspected Staph Outbreak," *Milwaukee Journal Sentinel*, October 3, 2003, p. 1B.

3. N. Gantz, et al., "Methicillin-Resistant *Staphylococcus aureus* Infections Among Competitive Sports Participants—Colorado, Indiana, Pennsylvania, and Los Angeles County, 2000–2003," *Morbidity and Mortality Weekly Report*, August 22, 2003, p. 793.

4. Michael LePage, "Superbug Strain Hits the Healthy," *New Scientist*, March 8, 2003, p. 4.

5. Daniel N. Yee, "Health Officials Warn of Antibiotic-Resistant Skin Infections among Athletes," *Associated Press State & Local Wire*, October 15, 2003 (accessed through LexisNexis Academic Universe, September 17, 2004). See also N. Gantz, et al.

6. T. Baba, et al., "Genome and Virulence Determinants of High Virulence Community-Acquired MRSA," *The Lancet*, May 25, 2003, p. 1819; Michael McCarthy, "Resistant Bacteria Spread Through U.S. Communities: 70% of Isolates Are Now Resistant to All β-lactam Antibiotics," *The Lancet*, November 8, 2003, p. 1554.

7. "*Staphylococcus aureus* Resistant to Vancomycin—United States, 2002," *Morbidity and Mortality Weekly Report*, July 5, 2002, p. 565; Makoto Kuroda, et al., "Whole Genome Sequencing of Methicillin-resistant *Staphylococcus aureus*," *The Lancet*, April 21, 2001, p. 1225.

8. Ramanan Laxminarayan and Mark Plotkin, "'Superbug' Threat," *Washington Post*, November 4, 2003, p. A25; Pamela Nolan, "Unclean Hands: Holding Hospitals Responsible for

Hospital-Acquired Infections," *Columbia Journal of Law & Social Problems*, Winter 2000, p. 133.

9. Roni Rabin, "Mysterious Crop of Staph: Newborns, Moms Infected after Stay at St. Catherine's," *Newsday*, October 9, 2003, p. A3.

10. Elinor Levy and Mark Fischetti, *The New Killer Diseases: How the Alarming Evolution of Mutant Germs Threatens Us All* (New York: Crown Publishers, 2003), p. 186.

11. Nicholas Graves, "Economics and Preventing Hospital-acquired Infection," *Emerging Infectious Diseases*, April 2004, p. 561; Nolan.

12. Bob Groves, "Still Searching for Kryptonite: Superbugs' March Prompts Expansion of a Testing and Database Program," *The Record* (Bergen County, N.J.), June 30, 2003, p. F1; World Health Organization, "The World Health Report 1996: Executive Summary," 1996, p. 4, <http://www.who.int/whr2001/2001/archives/1996/pdf/exsum96e.pdf> (June 2, 2004).

13. Laxminarayan and Plotkin; Nolan.

14. Randy Ludlow, "Wrongful Deaths. Inadequate Care. Questionable Doctors," *Columbus Dispatch*, August 24, 2003, p. 1A; Randy Ludlow, "Danger of Staph Outbreak Realized Too Late," *Columbus Dispatch*, May 20, 2003, p. 1A; Paul Souhrada, "Staph Cases More Widespread," *Columbus Dispatch*, May 6, 2003, p. 1C.

15. "Outbreaks of Community-Associated Methicillin-Resistant *Staphylococcus aureus* Skin Infections—Los Angeles County, California, 2002–2003," *Morbidity & Mortality Weekly Report*, February 7, 2002, p. 88.

16. James Surowiecki, "No Profit, No Cure," *The New Yorker*, November 5, 2001, p. 46; Roxanne Nelson, "Antibiotic Development Pipeline Runs Dry," *The Lancet*, November 22, 2003, p. 1726; Sebastian G. B. Amyes, *Magic Bullets, Lost Horizons: The Rise and Fall of Antibiotics* (London and New York: Taylor & Francis, 2001), p. 233.

17. World Health Organization, "The World Health Report 1996: Executive Summary," p. 1, 2001, <http://www.who.in/whr2001/2001/archives/1996/pdf/exsum96e.pdf> (June 2, 2004).

18. World Health Organization Report on Infectious Diseases 2000: Overcoming Antimicrobial Resistance, WHO/CDS/2000.2 Geneva

2000, Preface, 2000, <http://www.who.int/infectious-disease-report/2000/ index.html> (June 2, 2004).

19. "Study Shows Drug-Resistant Germs Are on the Rise," *Medical Letter on the CDC & FDA*, April 6, 2003, p. 9.

Chapter 2 Battle Against the "Bugs"

1. Population Reference Bureau, "2004 World Population Data Sheet," 2004, p. 5, <http://www.prb.org/pdf04/04WorldData Sheet_Eng.pdf> (January 18, 2005).

2. Comm Tech Lab, Michigan State University, "Microbe Zoo: Dirtland," 2000, <http://commtechlab.msu.edu/sites/dlc-me/zoo/zdmain.html> (January 18, 2005).

3. Dartmouth Medical School, "Intimate Strangers," 2004, <http://www.dartmouth.edu/dms/news/publications/dartmed/ spring00/html/intimate_strangers.shtml> (January 22, 2005).

4. David Tenenbaum, "Microbial Population Explosion," 1998, <http://whyfiles.org/shorties/count_bact.html> (January 18, 2005).

5. Thien-Fah Mah, et al., "A Genetic Basis for *Pseudomonas aeruginosa* Biofilm Antibiotic Resistance," *Nature*, November 20, 2003, p. 426; Georgia O'Toole, "A Resistance Switch," *Nature*, April 18, 2002, p. 695.

6. Stephen R. Palumbi, *The Evolution Explosion: How Humans Cause Rapid Evolutionary Change* (New York: W.W. Norton & Co., 2001), p. 67, discussing Psalm 51:7.

7. Kimberly M. Thompson with Debra Fulghum Bruce, *Overkill: How Our Nation's Abuse of Antibiotics and Other Germ Killers Is Hurting Your Health and What You Can Do About It* (Emmaus, Pa.: Rodale, 2002), p. 22.

8. "The Discovery of Penicillin," *Nobelprize.org*, 2003, <http:// nobelprize.org/medicine/educational/penicillin/readmore.html> (January 19, 2005); Stuart B. Levy, *The Antibiotic Paradox: How the Misuse of Antibiotics Destroys Their Curative Powers*, 2nd ed. (Cambridge, Mass.: Perseus Publishing, 2002), pp. 36–38; Michael Shnayerson and Mark J. Plotkin, *The Killers Within: The Deadly Rise of Drug-Resistant Bacteria* (Boston: Little, Brown & Co., 2002), pp. 32–33; Paul A. Offit, et al., *Breaking the Antibiotic*

Habit: A Parent's Guide to Coughs, Colds, Ear Infections, and Sore Throats (New York: John Wiley & Sons, Inc., 1999), p. 15.

9. Alexander Fleming, "On the Antibacterial Action of Cultures of a Penicillium, with Special Reference to Their Use in the Isolation of B. Influenzae," *The British Journal of Experimental Pathology*, 1929, p. 226, reprinted in Bulletin of the World Health Organization, 2001, pp. 780, 785.

10. Shnayerson and Plotkin, p. 34; Offit, pp. 15–16; Levy, pp. 43–35; Pete Moore, *Killer Germs: Rogue Diseases of the Twenty-First Century* (London: Carlton Books, 2001), pp. 57–58.

11. Offit, p. 16; Levy, pp. 1–2, 5–6, 43–45.

12. John S. Mailer, Jr., and Barbara Mason, "Penicillin," 2001, <http://www.lib.niu.edu/ipo/iht810139.html> (January 18, 2005).

13. Image C46-2-12_1948, provided courtesy of Pfizer, Inc.; Levy, p. 10; Moore, plate 13.

14. Carol L. Moberg and Zanvil A. Cohn, eds., *Launching the Antibiotic Era: Personal Accounts of the Discovery and Use of the First Antibiotics* (New York: Rockefeller University Press, 1990), p. 14; The Nobel Foundation, "The Nobel Prize in Physiology or Medicine 1952," 2003, <http://www. nobel.se/medicine/ laureates/1952/press.html> (August 31, 2004).

15. See generally Felissa R. Lashley and Jerry D. Durham, eds., *Emerging Infectious Diseases: Trends and Issues* (New York: Springer Publishing Company, 2002), pp. 27–28; National Institutes of Health, *Antimicrobial Resistance: Issues and Options* (Washington, D.C.: National Academy Press, 1998), p. 105.

16. Moore, p. 73; Palumbi, p. 92.

17. "Penicillin's Finder Assays Its Future," *New York Times*, June 26, 1945, p. 21.

18. Moberg and Cohn, p. 92.

19. Paul A. Tambyah, John A. Marx, and Dennis G. Maki, "Nosocomial Infection with Vancomycin-dependent Enterococci," *Emerging Infectious Diseases*, July 2004, p. 1277. See also Lashley and Durham, pp. 248–249.

20. A. J. Hostetler, "Drug-Resistant Flu Rate Surprises Testers," *Richmond Times Dispatch*, August 27, 2004, p. A11.

Chapter 3 Prescription for Trouble?

1. See, e.g., Fred Reinfeld, *Miracle Drugs and the New Age of Medicine* (New York: Sterling Publishing Co., Inc., 1957), p. 40.

2. Mark Rosenberg, "Taking Unnecessary Antibiotics Harmful in Long Run," *Chicago Daily Herald*, October 29, 2001, p. 4; Cheryl Clark and Scott LaFee, "Hospital Patients Face Growing Infection Peril," *San Diego Union-Tribune*, April 9, 2000, p. A1.

3. Linda F. McCaig, Richard E. Besser, and James M. Hughes, "Antimicrobial Drug Prescription in Ambulatory Care Settings, United States, 1992–2000," *Emerging Infectious Diseases*, April 2003, pp. 432, 434.

4. Personal telephone interview with John Powers, August 5, 2004. See also "Control of Antimicrobial Resistance: Time for Action," *British Medical Journal*, September 5, 1998, p. 612.

5. Jodi Vanden Eng, et al., "Consumer Attitudes and Use of Antibiotics," *Emerging Infectious Diseases*, September 2003, p. 1128; David Wahlberg, "Ads Aim To Curb Abuse of Antibiotics," *Atlanta Journal-Constitution*, September 18, 2003, p. 4A.

6. Reuters, "Experts Warn Lawmakers of Wave of 'Superbugs,'" *New York Times*, December 15, 1998, p. F10. See also Mariko Thompson, "Putting a Chill on Important Pills," *Daily News of Los Angeles*, November 10, 2003, Valley ed., p. U4; "Antimicrobial Drug Resistance: Is There an Answer?" *Consultant*, May 1999, p. 1376; Tamar Nordenberg, "Miracle Drugs vs. Superbugs," *FDA Consumer*, November 1998, p. 22.

7. Personal telephone interview with Richard Besser, August 6, 2004.

8. Ibid.

9. Public Health Image Library, Image 3647, <http://phil.cdc.gov/Phil/detail.asp?id=3647> (September 8, 2004).

10. Michael Barza and Karin Travers, "Excess Infections Due to Antimicrobial Resistance: The 'Attributable Fraction,'" *Clinical Infectious Diseases*, June 1, 2002, pp. S126, S12–S129.

11. See Amee R. Manges, et al., "Widespread Distribution of Urinary Tract Infections Caused by a Multidrug-Resistant *Escherichia Coli* Clonal Group," *New England Journal of Medicine*, October 4, 2001, p. 1007.

12. Michael Shnayerson and Mark J. Plotkin, *The Killers Within: The Deadly Rise of Drug-Resistant Bacteria* (Boston: Little, Brown & Co., 2002), p. 112; Ricki Lewis, "The Greatest Fear— Vancomycin Resistance," *FDA Consumer*, September 1995, <http://www.fda. gov/fdac/features/795_ antibio.html> (January 18, 2005).

13. Thomas F. O'Brien, "Emergence, Spread, and Environmental Effect of Antimicrobial Resistance: How Use of an Antimicrobial Anywhere Can Increase Resistance to Any Antimicrobial Anywhere Else," *Clinical Infectious Diseases*, June 1, 2002, p. S78.

14. Personal telephone interview with Stuart B. Levy, July 27, 2004.

15. Polly F. Harrison and Joshua Lederberg, eds., *Antimicrobial Resistance: Issues and Options* (Washington, D.C.: National Academy Press, 1998), p. 44 and n. 44.

16. Personal telephone interview with Richard Besser, August 6, 2004.

17. Ibid.

18. Harrison and Lederberg, pp. 44–45.

19. Cato Pedder, "Call for a 50 Per Cent Cut in Antibiotic Prescribing," *Pulse*, December 6, 2004, p. 3.

20. Harrison and Lederberg, pp. 44–46.

21. Ibid. See also Satinder Kumar, Paul Little, and Nicky Britten, "Why Do General Practitioners Prescribe Antibiotics for Sore Throat?" *British Medical Journal*, January 18, 2003, p. 138.

22. Personal telephone interview with Richard Besser, August 6, 2004.

23. Shnayerson and Plotkin, p. 287.

24. "Study Shows Drug-Resistant Germs Are on the Rise," Medical Letter on the CDC & FDA, April 6, 2003, p. 9.

25. American Academy of Pediatrics, "Questions and Answers on Acute Otitis Media," 2004, <http://www.aap.org/advocacy/ releases/aomqa.htm> (September 13, 2004).

26. American Academy of Pediatrics and American Academy of Family Physicians, "Diagnosis and Management of Acute Otitis Media," *Pediatrics*, May 2004, p. 1451, <http://aappolicy. aappublications.org/cgi/reprint/pediatrics;113/5/1451.pdf> (September 13, 2004). See also Mark H. Ebell, "Acute Otitis

Media in Children," *American Family Physician,* June 15, 2004,
p. 2896.

27. Personal telephone interview with John Powers, August 5, 2004.

28. Linda F. McCaig, Richard E. Besser, and James M. Hughes,
"Trends in Antimicrobial Prescribing Rates for Children and
Adolescents," *JAMA, Journal of the American Medical Association,*
June 19, 2002, p. 3096.

29. Linda F. McCaig, Richard E. Besser, and James M. Hughes,
"Antimicrobial Drug Prescriptions in Ambulatory Care Settings,
United States, 1992–2000," *Emerging Infectious Diseases,* April
2003, p. 432.

30. Personal telephone interview with Richard Besser, August 4, 2004.

31. John M. Boyce and Didier Pittet, "Guideline for Hand Hygiene in
Health-Care Settings," *Morbidity and Mortality Weekly Report,*
October 25, 2002, pp. 1, 22. See also "Come Clean," *Nursing
Standard,* August 18, 2004, p. 22.

32. Boyce and Pittet, pp. 26–28.

33. Belinda E. Ostrowsky, et al., "Control of Vancomycin-Resistant
Enterococcus in Health Care Facilities in a Region," *New England
Journal of Medicine,* May 10, 2001, p. 1427.

34. See Robert Weinstein, "Controlling Antimicrobial Resistance in
Hospitals: Infection Control and Use of Antibiotics," *Emerging
Infectious Diseases,* March–April 2001, pp. 188, 190. See also Elinor
Levy and Mark Fischetti, *The New Killer Diseases: How the
Alarming Evolution of Mutant Germs Threatens Us All* (New York:
Crown Publishers, 2003), p. 188.

35. Michael A. Misocky, "The Epidemic of Antibiotic Resistance: A
Legal Remedy To Eradicate the 'Bugs' in the Treatment of
Infectious Diseases," *Akron Law Review,* 1997, pp. 733, 744–766.

36. Personal telephone interview with Stuart B. Levy, July 27, 2004.

37. Personal telephone interview with John Powers, August 5, 2004.

Chapter 4 Not Just What the Doctor Ordered

1. Stuart B. Levy, *The Antibiotic Paradox: How the Misuse of
Antibiotics Endangers Their Curative Powers* (Reading, Mass.:
Oxford Perseus, 2002), p. 152.

2. Michael Shnayerson and Mark J. Plotkin, *The Killers Within: the Deadly Rise of Drug-Resistant Bacteria* (Boston: Little, Brown & Co., 2002), pp. 52–53; Levy, pp. 150–151.

3. Animal Health Institute, "The Antibiotics Debate: Antibiotics and Safe Food," 2002, <http://www.ahi.org/antibioticsDebate/ antibioticsandsafefood.asp> (September 3, 2004).

4. Union of Concerned Scientists, "Hogging It! Estimates of Antimicrobial Abuse in Livestock," January 2001, Appendix C, <http://www.ucsusa.org/documents/hog_apps.pdf> (September 3, 2004).

5. General Accounting Office, "Antibiotic Resistance: Federal Agencies Need to Better Focus Efforts to Address Risk to Humans from Antibiotic Use in Animals," GAO–04–490, April 2004, p. 39.

6. Peter Radetsky, "Last Days of the Wonder Drugs," *Discover*, November 1998, p. 76.

7. Katherine M. Shea, "Nontherapeutic Use of Antimicrobial Agents in Animal Agriculture: Implications for Pediatrics," *Pediatrics*, September 2004, p. 862.

8. Union of Concerned Scientists, "Hogging It! Estimates of Antimicrobial Abuse in Livestock," January 2001, Executive Summary, <http://www.ucsusa.org/food_and_environment/ antibiotic_resistance/page.cfm?pageID=264> (September 3, 2004).

9. Levy, p. 152.

10. See, e.g., Nicole M. Iovine and Martin J. Blaser, "Antibiotics in Animal Feed and Spread of Resistant Campylobacter from Poultry to Humans," *Emerging Infectious Diseases*, June 1, 2004, p. 1158.

11. Animal Health Institute, "The Antibiotics Debate: Antibiotics and Safe Food," 2002, <http://www.ahi.org/antibioticsDebate/ antibioticsandsafefood.asp> (September 3, 2004); John Fauber, "The Perils of Animal Antibiotics," *Milwaukee Journal Sentinel*, November 4, 2001, p. 1A.

12. Anne K. Vidaver, "Uses of Antimicrobials in Plant Agriculture," *Clinical Infectious Diseases*, May 2002, p. S107; Patricia S. McManus, "Antibiotic Use for Plant Disease Management in the United States," *Plant Health Progress*, March 27, 2001,

<http://www.apsnet.org/education/feature/antibiotic/top.htm>
(September 5, 2004).

13. Food and Drug Administration, Docket 00N–1571, Initial
Decision, March 16, 2004, p. 46, <http://www.fda.gov/ohrms/
dockets/dailys/04/mar04/031604/00n-1571-idf0001-vol389.pdf>
(September 15, 2004); Felissa Lashley and Jerry D. Durham, eds.,
Emerging Infectious Diseases: Trends and Issues (New York: Springer
Publishing Company, 2002), p. 58.

14. General Accounting Office, p. 24.

15. Iovine and Blaser.

16. Ellen K. Silbergeld and Polly Walker, "What If Cipro Stopped
Working?" *New York Times*, November 3, 2001, p. A23.

17. Food and Drug Administration.

18. Shnayerson and Plotkin, pp. 53–54.

19. Paul D. Fey, et al., "Ceftriaxone-Resistant Salmonella Infection
Acquired by a Child from Cattle," *New England Journal of
Medicine*, April 27, 2000, p. 1242.

20. David G. White, et al., "The Isolation of Antibiotic-Resistant
Salmonella from Retail Ground Meats," *New England Journal of
Medicine*, October 18, 2001, p. 1147.

21. Compare Centers for Disease Control and Prevention, "Frequently
Asked Questions About Food Irradiation," 1999, <http://www.cdc.
gov/ncidod/dbmd/diseaseinfo/foodirradiation.htm> (January 19,
2005), with William Au, "Expert Affidavit on Safety of Irradiated
Food," October 28, 2001, <http://www.citizen.org/cmep/
foodsafety/food_irrad/articles.cfm?ID=6516> (January 19, 2005).

22. Heidi Splete, "Resistance Found Despite No Exposure to
Antibiotic," *Family Practice News*, December 15, 2003, p. 36.

23. Henrik C. Wegener, et al., "Use of Antimicrobial Growth
Promoters in Food Animals and *Enterococcus faecium* Resistance to
Therapeutic Antimicrobial Drugs in Europe," *Emerging Infectious
Diseases*, May 1, 1999, p. 23.

24. Ben Ridwan, et al., "What Actions Should Be Taken To Prevent
Spread of Vancomycin Resistant Enterococci in European
Hospitals?" *British Medical Journal*, March 16, 2002, p. 666.

25. Shnayerson and Plotkin, pp. 92–93, 98, 103, 112; Chris Adams,

"FDA Approves Rhone-Poulenc Superbug Drug," *Wall Street Journal*, September 22, 1999, p. B7.

26. L. Clifford McDonald, et al., "Quinupristin-Dalfopristin-Resistant *Enterococcus Faecium* on Chicken and in Human Stool Specimens," *New England Journal of Medicine*, October 18, 2001, p. 1155; Marc Kaufman, "Worries Rise over Effect of Antibiotics in Animal Feed," *Washington Post*, March 17, 2000, p. A1.

27. L. A. Welton, et al., "Antimicrobial Resistance in Enterococci Isolated from Turkey Flocks Fed Virginiamycin," *Antimicrobial Agents & Chemotherapy*, March 1998, p. 705; Laura E. Kehoe, et al., "Structural Basis of Synercid® (Quinupristin-Salfopristin) Resistance in Gram-positive Bacterial Pathogens," *Journal of Biological Chemistry*, August 8, 2003, p. 29963. See also General Accounting Office, "Antibiotic Resistance: Federal Agencies Need to Better Focus Efforts to Address Risk to Humans from Antibiotic Use in Animals," GAO–04–490, April 2004, p. 25.

28. Animal Health Institute, "The Antibiotics Debate," 2002, <http://www. ahi.org/antibioticsDebate/index.asp> (September 3, 2004).

29. Sebastian G. B. Amyes, *Magic Bullets, Lost Horizons: The Rise and Fall of Antibiotics* (London and New York: Taylor & Francis, 2001), p. 158. See also Ian Phillips, et al., "Does the Use of Antibiotics in Food Animals Pose a Risk to Human Health?" *Journal of Antimicrobial Chemotherapy*, January 2004, p. 28; Q. A. McKellar, "Antimicrobial Resistance: A Veterinary Perspective," *British Medical Journal*, September 5, 1998, p. 610.

30. Elinor Levy and Mark Fischetti, *The New Killer Diseases: How the Alarming Evolution of Mutant Germs Threatens Us All* (New York: Crown Publishers, 2003), p. 195; Pete Moore, *Killer Germs: Rogue Diseases of the Twenty-First Century* (London: Carlton Books, 2001), p. 94.

31. Henrik Wegener, "Casting Pills Before Swine," *Newsweek*, January 22, 2001, p. 2.

32. Animal Health Institute, "The Antibiotics Debate," 2002, <http://www. ahi.org/antibioticsDebate/index.asp> (September 3, 2004); Ian Phillips, et al., pp. 28, 42–44; Animal Health Institute, "European Experience Withdrawing Antibiotic Growth Promoters

Use," 2002, <http://www.ahi.org/mediaCenter/mediaKit/
EUExperienceWithdraw.asp> (January 22, 2005).

33. General Accounting Office, p. 25.

34. See, e.g., Kenneth H. Mathews, Jr., "Antimicrobial Drug Use and
Veterinary Costs in U.S. Livestock Production," U.S. Department
of Agriculture, Economic Research Service, Bulletin 766, May
2001.

35. See, e.g., "Preservation of Antibiotics for Medical Treatment
Act of 2003," S. 1560, 108th Congress, 1st Sess., introduced
July 25, 2003; H.R. 2932, 108th Congress, 1st Sess., introduced
July 25, 2003.

36. Marian Burros, "Poultry Industry Quietly Cuts Back on Antibiotic
Use," *New York Times*, February 10, 2002, sec. 1, p. 1. See also
Center for Science in the Public Interest, "CSPI Applauds Tyson,
Foster Farms, and Perdue for Not Fattening Chickens with
Medically Important Antibiotics," press release, February 11,
2002, <http://www.cspinet.org/new/antibiotics02_11_02.html>
(September 4, 2004).

37. Marc Kaufman, "McDonald's Will Tell Meat Suppliers To Cut
Antibiotics Use," *Washington Post*, June 19, 2003, p. A3;
"McDonald's Calls for Phase-Out of Growth Promoting Antibiotics
in Meat Supply, Establishes Global Policy on Antibiotic Use," Press
release, June 19, 2003, <http://www.mcdonalds.com/corp/news/
corppr/pr06192003. html> (September 3, 2004); "McDonald's
Global Policy on Antibiotic Use in Food Animals," June 3, 2003,
<http://www.mcdonalds.com/corp/values/socialrespons/market/
antibiotics/global_policy.html> (July 20, 2004).

38. See, e.g., Richard J. Heath and Charles O. Rock, "A
Triclosan-Resistant Bacterial Enzyme," *Nature*, July 13, 2000,
p. 145.

39. Stuart B. Levy, "Antibacterial Household Products: Cause for
Concern," *Emerging Infectious Diseases*, June 2001 supplement,
pp. 512, 513-14; Rungtip Chuanchuen, et al., "Cross-Resistance
between Triclosan and Antibiotics in *Pseudomonas aeruginosa* Is
Mediated by Multidrug Efflux Pumps: Exposure of a Susceptible
Mutant Strain to Triclosan Selects *nfxB* Mutants Overexpressing
MexCD-OprJ," *Antimicrobial Agents and Chemotherapy*, February

2001, p. 428; A. D. Russell, et al., "Possible Link between Bacterial Resistance and Use of Antibiotics and Biocides," *Antimicrobial Agents and Chemotherapy*, August 1998, p. 2151; "Antibacterial Overkill," *Tufts University Health & Nutrition Letter*, October 1998, p. 1.

40. Personal telephone interview with Stuart B. Levy, July 27, 2004.

41. Jane E. Brody, "How Germ-Phobia Can Lead to Illness," *New York Times*, June 20, 2000, p. F8.

42. Personal telephone interview with Stuart B. Levy, July 27, 2004.

43. Ibid.

44. The Soap and Detergent Association, "Some FAQs About Bacterial Resistance From Antibacterial Wash Products," n.d., <http://www.cleaning101.com/health/faq.html> (September 2, 2004).

45. Peter Gilbert and Andrew McBain, "Live and Let Die," *Microbiology Today*, May 2004, pp. 62–63.

46. Personal telephone interview with George Fischler, September 20, 2004.

47. E. C. Cole, et al., "Investigation of Antibiotic and Antibacterial Agent Cross-Resistance in Target Bacteria from Homes of Antibacterial Product Users and Nonusers," *Journal of Applied Microbiology*, October 2003, p. 664; Lois M. Collins, "Antibacterial Soap Won't Create 'Super Bugs,'" *Deseret Morning News*, September 24, 2003, p. A1. See also A. D. Russell, "Whither Triclosan?" *Journal of Antimicrobial Chemotherapy*, May 2004, p. 693.

48. Personal telephone interview with George Fischler, September 20, 2004.

49. Ibid. See also The Soap and Detergent Association, "Cleaning for Health: Benefits of Handwashing and Antibacterial Soaps," n.d., <http://www.cleaning101.com/health/health/cleaninghealth8.html> (September 7, 2004); The Soap and Detergent Association, Comments to Food and Drug Administration, Docket No. 75N–183H, August 27, 2003, <http://www.fda.gov/ohrms/dockets/dailys/03/Sept03/090303/75n-0183h-000084-01-vol167.pdf> (September 7, 2004).

50. Janet Raloff, "Pharm Pollution: Excreted Antibiotics Can Poison Plants," *Science News*, June 29, 2002, p. 406.

51. Dana W. Kolpin, et al., "Pharmaceuticals, Hormones, and Other Organic Wastewater Contaminants in U.S. Streams, 1999–2000: A National Reconnaissance," *Environmental Science & Technology*, March 15, 2002, p. 1202; Britt E. Erickson, "Analyzing the Ignored Environmental Contaminants," *Environmental Science & Technology*, April 1, 2002, p. 140A. See generally Christopher T. Nidel, "Regulating the Fate of Pharmaceutical Drugs: A New Prescription for the Environment," *Food and Drug Law Journal*, 2003, pp. 81, 83–90.

52. International Joint Commission, Twelfth Biennial Report on Great Lakes Water Quality, September 2004, p. 30, <http://www.ijc.org/php/publications/html/12br/pdf/12thbrfull_e.pdf> (January 19, 2005); Ronnie B. Levin, et al., "U.S. Drinking Water Challenges in the Twenty-First Century," *Environmental Health Perspectives*, February 2002, pp. 43, 47.

53. Tom Pelton, "Poultry Farms' Use of Antibiotics Raises Concerns about Drug-Resistant Germs," *Baltimore Sun*, August 31, 2004, p. 1A.

54. Richard Lobb and Ronn Phillips, "Use of Antibiotics in Animals Is Safe," *Baltimore Sun*, September 11, 2004, p. 13A.

Chapter 5   Special Problems

1. See "AIDS Therapy: FDA-Approved Study Launched to Treat AIDS Patients in Virologic Failure," Medical Letter on the CDC & FDA, May 23, 2004, p. 7. See also Stephen R. Palumbi, *The Evolution Explosion: How Humans Cause Rapid Evolutionary Change* (New York: W.W. Norton & Co., 2001), pp. 119–126.

2. "Drug-Resistance Guide Being Pondered by CDC," *AIDS Alert*, November 2003, p. 146.

3. Geoffrey Cowley, "Medicine without Doctors," *Newsweek*, July 19, 2004, p. 44; Lawrence K. Altman, "AIDS Drugs' Fast Rise in Asia Risks Resistant Strains," *New York Times*, July 8, 2004, p. A3; "Mutated Strains of AIDS Feared," *Seattle Post-Intelligencer*, July 8, 2004, p. A5. See also World Health Organization, "Drug Resistance Threatens to Reverse Medical Progress," Press release WHO/41, June 12, 2000 <http://www.who.int/inf-pr-2000/en/pr2000-41.html> (August 16, 2004).

4. Nick Schulz, "Resistance Is Deadly," *National Review Online*, March 22, 2004 (accessed through LEXIS/NEXIS Academic Universe, August 1, 2004); Lee B. Reichman with Janice Hopkins Tanne, *Timebomb: The Global Epidemic of Multi-Drug-Resistant Tuberculosis* (New York: McGraw-Hill, 2002), pp. 43–46.

5. Matthew Gandy and Alimuddin Zumla, eds., *The Return of the White Plague: Global Poverty and the 'New' Tuberculosis* (London: Verso, 2003), p. 95; Reichman and Tanne, pp. x, 11–12; Felisha R. Lashley and Jerry D. Durham, eds., *Emerging Infectious Diseases: Trends and Issues* (New York: Springer Publishing Company, 2002), p. 204.

6. Tennessee Department of Health, "Tuberculosis," n.d., <http://www2.state.tn.us/health/FactSheets/tb.htm> (January 22, 2005); Los Angeles Department of Health, "Tuberculosis Epidemiology Update," 1999, <http://www.lapublichealth.org/tb/faq/99Facts/99fact.htm> (January 22, 2005).

7. Kimberly M. Thompson with Debra Fulghum Bruce, *Overkill: How Our Nation's Abuse of Antibiotics and Other Germ Killers Is Hurting Your Health and What You Can Do About It* (Emmaus, Pa.: Rodale Press, 2002), p. 31.

8. Reichman and Tanne, pp. 36–38.

9. Stuart B. Levy, *The Antibiotic Paradox: How the Misuse of Antibiotics Endangers Their Curative Powers* (Reading, Mass.: Oxford Perseus, 2002), pp. 107–108; Reichman and Tanne, pp. ix, 46–47.

10. Robert McFadden, "A Drug-Resistant TB Results in 13 Deaths in New York Prisons," *New York Times*, November 16, 1991, pp. A1, A22. See also Elisabeth Rosenthal, "Doctors Warn of a Looming TB Threat," *New York Times*, November 16, 1991, p. 22.

11. Levy, pp. 107–108; Reichman and Tanne, p. ix.

12. Gandy and Zumla, p. 35.

13. Palumbi, pp. 86–87; Lashley and Durham, pp. 208–210.

14. James K. Glassman, "TB: Good News, Bad News, Good News," *Saturday Evening Post*, July–August 2004, p. 74; Schulz.

15. World Health Organization, "Drug- and Multidrug-Resistant Tuberculosis (MDR–TB)—Frequently Asked Questions,"

2005, <http://www.who.int/tb/dots/dotsplus/faq/en/> (January 22, 2005).

16. Ganapati Mudur, "Medical Charity Criticizes Shortcomings of DOTS in Management of Tuberculosis," *British Medical Journal,* April 3, 2004, p. 784.

17. Michael Hopkin, "WHO Urges World to Fight TB 'Super-strains,'" Nature Science Update, March 16, 2004, <http://www.nature.com/nsu/nsu_pf/040315/041315-3.html> (March 23, 2004).

18. Reichman and Tanne, p. 53.

19. Ibid., p. 54.

20. Ibid., p. 115.

21. Gandy and Zumla, pp. 208–209.

22. Reichman and Tanne, p. 34; Santa Clara County Public Health Department, "Tuberculin Skin Testing of BCG-Vaccinated Persons," September 2000, <http://www.scvmed.org/scc/assets/docs/110733TB Factsheet1E.pdf> (January 22, 2005).

23. Stop TB, "Tuberculosis: The Worsening Epidemic," n.d., <http://w3.whosea.org/tb/pdf/kit/right7.pdf> (January 22, 2005); Reichman and Tanne, p. xi; Lashley and Durham, p. 204.

24. University of Leicester, "Malaria: History and Distribution," October 22, 2004, <http://www-micro.msb.le.ac.uk/224/Bradley/History.html> (January 19, 2005); Global Health Council, "Malaria: Africa's Time Bomb," 2002, <http://www.globalhealth.org/news/article/1933> (January 19, 2005).

25. Christine Gorman, "Death by Mosquito," *Time,* July 26, 2004, p. 50.

26. Pascoal Mocumbi, "Plague of My People," *Nature,* August 19, 2004, p. 925; "Four Horsemen of the Apocalypse?" *The Economist,* May 3, 2003 (U.S. edition), p. NA (accessed through InfoTrac OneFile, January 22, 2005).

27. Paul M. O'Neill, "A Worthy Adversary for Malaria," *Nature,* August 19, 2004, p. 838; Brian Greenwood, "Between Hope and a Hard Place," *Nature,* August 19, 2004, p. 926; Gorman; Anita Manning, "Report Urges a New War on Malaria," *USA Today,* July 21, 2004, p. 9D.

28. Michael Shnayerson and Mark J. Plotkin, *The Killers Within: The*

Deadly Rise of Drug-Resistant Bacteria (Boston: Little, Brown & Co., 2002), pp. 211–214; Pete Moore, *Killer Germs: Rogue Diseases of the Twenty-First Century* (London: Carlton Books, 2001), pp. 33–34; "Plague in Madagascar—Maybe Closer, Maybe Soon?" *Infectious Disease Alert*, April 1, 2000, p. 98.

29. United Nations Office on Drugs and Crime, "Biological Weapons: What's What," 2004, <http://www.unodc.org/unodc/terrorism_weapons_mass_destruction_page005.html> (January 19, 2005); Wendy Orent, *Plague: The Mysterious Past and Terrifying Future of the World's Most Dangerous Disease* (New York: Free Press, 2004), pp. 211–233.

30. Centers for Disease Control and Prevention, "Frequently Asked Questions (FAQ) About Plague," July 27, 2004, <http://www.bt.cdc.gov/agent/plague/faq.asp> (January 19, 2005).

31. Centers for Disease Control and Prevention, "Smallpox Disease Overview," December 30, 2004, <http://www.bt.cdc.gov/agent/smallpox/overview/disease-facts.asp> (January 19, 2005).

32. Edward A. Belongia, et al., "Demand for Prophylaxis after Bioterrorism-related Anthrax Cases, 2001," *Emerging Infectious Diseases*, January 2005, p. 42; Douglas Shaffer, et al., "Increased US Prescription Trends Associated with the CDC *Bacillus anthracis* Antimicrobial Postexposure Prophylaxis Campaign," *Pharmacoepidemiology and Drug Safety*, April–May 2003, p. 177; Alexander C. Tsai, et al., "An Outbreak of Web Sites Selling Ciprofloxacin Following an Outbreak of Anthrax by Mail," *American Journal of Medicine*, October 1, 2002, p. 424; Raja Mishra, "Cipro Use Troubles Some Specialists," *Boston Globe*, December 16, 2001, p. A18; "Hoarding Cipro," *New York Times*, October 17, 2001.

Chapter 6 Seeking Solutions

1. Personal telephone interview with Stuart B. Levy, July 27, 2004.

2. Compare Polly F. Harrison and Joshua Lederberg, eds., *Antimicrobial Resistance: Issues and Options* (Washington, D.C.: National Academy Press, 1998), p. 60, with Roxanne Nelson, "Antibiotic Development Pipeline Runs Dry," *The Lancet*, November 22, 2003, p. 1726.

3. Personal telephone interview with Stuart B. Levy, July 27, 2004.

4. Personal telephone interview with John Powers, August 5, 2004.

5. Ibid.; Richard P. Wenzel, "The Antibiotic Pipeline—Challenges, Costs, and Values," *New England Journal of Medicine*, August 5, 2004, p. 523.

6. Scott Hensley, "New Antibiotic Could Boost Besieged Aventis," *Wall Street Journal*, March 4, 2004, p. B1.

7. See generally FDA, "From Test Tube to Patient: Improving Health Through Human Drugs," September 1999, <http://www.fda.gov/cder/about/whatwedo/testtube-full.pdf> (August 25, 2004). See also Wyeth Pharmaceuticals, "Drug Approval Process," 2004, <http://www.wyeth.com/education/approval.asp> (July 28, 2004).

8. Personal telephone interview with Steven Projan, August 6, 2004.

9. Ibid. See also "Wyeth Pharmaceuticals: Pharmaceutical Company Seeks Global Regulatory Approval of Antibiotic," *Law & Health Weekly*, January 15, 2005, p. 476.

10. Wenzel. See also John H. Powers, "Development of Drugs for Antimicrobial-resistant Pathogens," *Current Opinion in Infectious Diseases*, December 2003, p. 547.

11. Personal telephone interview with Steven Projan, August 6, 2004.

12. Ibid.; personal telephone interview with Stuart B. Levy, July 27, 2004.

13. Della Deme, "Rib-X Pharmaceuticals: A Promising Biotech Startup," *Yale Entrepreneur*, Spring 2003, p. 20, <http://www.rib-x.com/YE.pdf> (August 24, 2004). See also National Community Pharmacists Association, "Rx Headlines, " January 24, 2003, <http://www.ncpanet.org/news_press/rx_headlines/2003/january/01.24.03> (September 23, 2004).

14. Personal telephone interview with Richard Besser, August 6, 2004; "New Vaccine Reduces Antibiotic-Resistant Infections and Protects Families," *Medical Letter on the CDC & FDA*, October 12, 2003, p. 5.

15. Anita Manning, "Vaccine Helps the Unvaccinated," *USA Today*, May 4, 2004, p. 1D.

16. Nabi Biopharmaceuticals, "Nabi Biopharmaceuticals Completes Patient Enrollment for StaphVAX® Phase III Trial and Completes Consistency Lot Manufacturing," press release, August 17, 2004,

<http://phx.corporate-ir.net/phoenix.zhtml?c=100445&p=
irol-newsArticle&ID=604600&highlight=> (March 2, 2005);
Amy Ellis Nutt, "Looking for a Vaccine," *The Star-Ledger*
(Newark), December 10, 2003, p. 14; Henry Shrinefield, et al.,
"Use of a *Stapholococcus Aureus* Conjugate Vaccine in Patients
Receiving Hemodialysis," *New England Journal of Medicine*,
February 14, 2002, p. 491.

17. Nabi Biopharmaceuticals, "Nabi Biopharmaceuticals Awarded
    Patent on Enterococcus Antigens and Vaccines," press release,
    August 10, 2004, <http://phx.corporate-ir.net/phoenix.zhtml?c=
    100445&p=irol-newsArticle&t=Regular&id=602759&>
    (March 2, 2005).

18. Elad Ziv, Charles L. Daley, and Sally Blower, "Potential Public
    Health Impact of New Tuberculosis Vaccines," *Emerging Infectious
    Diseases*, September 2004, p. 1529.

19. Michael Shnayerson and Mark J. Plotkin, *The Killers Within: The
    Deadly Rise of Drug-Resistant Bacteria* (Boston: Little, Brown &
    Co., 2002), pp. 169–171; John K. McCormick, Jeremy Yarwood,
    and Patrick Schlievert, "Toxic Shock Syndrome and Bacterial
    Superantigens," *Annual Review of Microbiology*, 2001, p. 77. On
    IVIG generally, see ITPkids.org, "Intravenous Immunoglobulin
    (IVIG)," 2002, <http://www.itpkids.org/docs/ivig.html>
    (January 19, 2005).

20. See, e.g., M. Zasloff, "Antimicrobial Peptides in Health and
    Disease," *New England Journal of Medicine*, October 10, 2002,
    p. 1199; Tomas Ganz, "Rings of Destruction," *Nature*, July 26,
    2001, p. 412.

21. Amy Ellis Nutt, "The Search for Answers," *The Star-Ledger*
    (Newark), December 10, 2003, p. 11; Mark Cheater, "Chasing the
    Magic Dragon," *National Wildlife Online*, August–September 2003,
    <http://www.nwf.org/nationalwildlife/article.cfm?articleid=
    810&issueid=63> (January 19, 2005); Gill Diamond, "Nature's
    Antibiotics—the Potential of Antimicrobial Peptides as New Drugs,"
    Biologist, October 2001, pp. 209–212.

22. Frank R. Stermitz, et al., "Synergy in a Medicinal Plant:
    Antimicrobial Action of Berberine Potentiated by 5*-
    Methoxyhydnocarpin, a Multidrug Pump Inhibitor," *Proceedings of*

the National Academy of Science (PNAS), February 15, 2000, p. 1433, <http://www.atsweb.neu.edu/lewislab/publications/ Sterm.pdf> (August 26, 2004). See also Mairin Brennan, "Plant May Hold Key to Ultimate Antibiotic," *Chemical & Engineering News,* February 21, 2000, p. 6.

23. "Garlic Compound Effective against Killer MRSA 'Superbugs,'" *Drug Week,* January 16, 2004, p. 6; Felissa R. Lashley and Jerry D. Durham, eds., *Emerging Infectious Diseases: Trends and Issues* (New York: Springer Publishing Company, 2002), p. 25.

24. Elinor Levy and Mark Fischetti, *The New Killer Diseases: How the Alarming Evolution of Mutant Germs Threatens Us All* (New York: Crown Publishers, 2003), p. 185; George T. Macfarlane and John H. Cummings, "Probiotics and Prebiotics: Can Regulating the Activities of All Intestinal Bacteria Benefit Health?" *British Medical Journal,* April 10, 1999, p. 999.

25. ConjuGon, "ConjuGon: Developing Fundamentally New Ways To Combat Bacterial Infection," 2003, <http://www.conjugon .com> (January 19, 2005); ConjuGon, "Patent Granted; Could Lead to New Antibiotic," November 19, 2003, <http://www. conjugon.com/news_story.php?id=18> (January 19, 2005); Jason Gertzen, "New Madison, Wis., Biotech Start-Up to Fight Antibiotic-Resistant Infections," *Milwaukee Journal Sentinel,* August 18, 2002, (accessed through LEXIS/NEXIS Academic Universe, August 24, 2004).

26. Nutt, "The Search for Answers," p. 11.

27. Personal telephone interview with Elizabeth Kutter, September 13, 2004.

28. John Travis, "All the World's a Phage: Viruses That Eat Bacteria Abound—and Surprise," and "Phages Behaving Badly: Viruses Can Control How Dangerous Some Bacteria Are," *Science News,* July 12, 2003, p. 26.

29. Evergreen State University, "Alfred's Story," n.d., <http://www. evergreen.edu/phage/phagetherapy/alfred.htm> (January 22, 2005); Amy Ellis Nutt, "Germs That Fight Germs: How Killer Bacteria Have Defeated Our Last Antibiotic," *The Star-Ledger* (Newark), December 9, 2003, p. 18; Shnayerson and Plotkin, pp. 234–236.

30. Personal telephone interview with Elizabeth Kutter, September 13, 2004.

31. Jascha Hoffman, "Revival of an Old Cure: Bacteria-Eating Viruses," *New York Times*, May 18, 2004, p. F7; David Stipp, "PhageTech: Biotech," *Fortune*, May 17, 2004, p. 142; Jane Bradbury, "'My Enemy's Enemy Is My Friend': Using Phages To Fight Bacteria," *The Lancet*, February 21, 2004, p. 624; Richard Stone, "Stalin's Forgotten Cure: Bacteriophage Therapy, Pioneered in Stalin-era Russia, Is Attracting Renewed Attention in the West as a Potential Weapon against Drug-resistant Bugs and Hard-to-treat Infections," *Science*, October 25, 2002, p. 728.

32. Personal telephone interview with Elizabeth Kutter, September 13, 2004.

33. See, e.g., Jing Liu, et al., "Antimicrobial Drug Discovery through Bacteriophage Genomics," *Nature Biotechnology*, January 11, 2004, p. 185.

Chapter 7   Time for Decisions

1. Pete Moore, *Killer Germs: Rogue Diseases of the Twenty-First Century* (London: Carlton Books, 2001), p. 25.

2. Marilynn Marchione, "Panel Warns of Microbial Outbreak," *Milwaukee Journal Sentinel*, March 19, 2003, p. 2A.

3. Karen Auge, "Stronger Strain of Gonorrhea Alarms CDC," *Denver Post*, May 2, 2004, p. A27; Rob Stein, "Drug Resistant Gonorrhea on the Rise," *Washington Post*, April 30, 2004, p. A8;

4. Pak-Leung Ho, et al., "Fluoroquinolone and Other Antimicrobial Resistance in Invasive Penumococci, Hong Kong, 1995–2001," *Emerging Infectious Diseases*, July 2004, p. 1250.

5. World Health Organization, "Drug Resistance Threatens To Reverse Medical Progress," Press release WHO/41, June 12, 2000, <http://www.who.int/inf-pr-2000/en/pr2000-41.html> (August 16, 2004). See also Stephan Harbarth and Matthew H. Samore, "Antimicrobial Resistance Determinants and Future Control," *Emerging Infectious Diseases*, June 2005, p. 794.

6. "Biological, Chemical, and Radiological Weapons Countermeasures Research Act," S. 666, 108th Congress, 1st Sess., introduced March 19, 2003 (not enacted).

7. Compare Nicholas Graves, "Economics and Preventing Hospital-acquired Infection," *Emerging Infectious Diseases,* April 2004, p. 561; with Bob Groves, "Still Searching for Kryptonite: Superbugs' March Prompts Expansion of a Testing and Database Program," *The Record* (Bergen County, NJ), June 30, 2003, p. F1.

8. Michael Shnayerson and Mark J. Plotkin, *The Killers Within: The Deadly Rise of Drug-Resistant Bacteria* (Boston: Little, Brown & Co., 2002), p. 113.

9. *Reynolds* v. *Goord,* 103 F. Supp. 2d 316, 334 & n. 31 (S.D.N.Y. 2000).

10. Guido S. Weber, "Unresolved Issues in Controlling the Tuberculosis Epidemic Among the Foreign-Born in the United States," *American Journal of Law and Medicine,* 1996, pp. 503, 524–525.

11. Lawrence O. Gostin, "Tuberculosis and the Power of the State: Toward the Development of Rational Standards for the Review of Compulsory Public Health Powers," University of Chicago Law School Roundable, 1995, p. 219; Karen S. Rothenberg and Elizabeth C. Lovoy, "Something Old, Something New: The Challenge of Tuberculosis Control in the Age of AIDS," *Buffalo Law Review,* Fall 1994, p. 715.

12. Personal telephone interview with Richard Besser, August 6, 2004.

Glossary

antibiotics—Substances that kill or stop the growth of bacteria. Initially, the term referred to a substance derived from natural organisms, such as molds or bacteria; now the term generally includes a range of synthetic, or manufactured, drugs too.

antimicrobials—Substances that kill or stop the growth or other functions of microbes.

bacteria—Single-celled living organisms that lack a separate cell nucleus.

bacteriophage—A virus that targets bacteria as its host.

broad-spectrum antibiotic—A drug that kills or inhibits many types of bacteria.

community-based—Referring to an infection that someone acquires in the community, as opposed to an institutional setting.

conjugation—In reference to bacteria, a method by which a bacterium transfers plasmid DNA to other cells.

daughter cells—Offspring of single-celled organisms after they go through cell division.

DNA—Deoxyribonucleic acid, the chemical that encodes genetic information in chromosomes.

growth promoters—Tiny doses of antibiotics added to animal feed or water with the goal of speeding growth and/or maintaining health for animals raised in confined areas.

host—An organism in or on which microbes live.

immune system—The body's natural defense mechanisms against disease.

inert—Inactive, dormant.

microbe—A microscopic organism that is too small to see without a microscope. Examples include bacteria, viruses, and some fungi and parasites.

MRSA—Methicillin-resistant *Staphylococcus aureus*, a drug-resistant bacteria that causes many hospital-based infections and increasing numbers of community-acquired infections.

nosocomial—Referring to an infection caught or acquired in a hospital or other health care setting.

parasite—An organism that lives in or on another living thing without giving its host any benefit.

pathogen—A microbe that causes disease.

peptide—Certain groupings of amino acids. Peptides play a part in fighting off various infections as part of the immune system.

plasmid—A ringlike piece of DNA outside a bacteria's nuclei that carries genetic information. Various plasmids carry genes for resisting antibiotics.

resistant—Hardy, or unaffected by something. Drug-resistant microbes can survive dosages of drugs that usually work against an infection.

selective pressure—Phenomenon where antibiotics or other drugs inadvertently encourage development of resistance. By killing off the most susceptible microbes, they "select" those that can survive.

superbug—A strain of infection that resists many different medications.

susceptible—Vulnerable, or likely to succumb. Bacteria that are readily killed by an antibiotic are susceptible to it.

therapeutic—Healing or curative; treating disease. A therapeutic dose is the amount of medicine needed to treat disease.

vaccine—Medication that provides immunity against a disease.

virus—A type of microbe that cannot grow or reproduce except when it infects a living organism's cells.

For More Information

Alliance for the Prudent Use of Antibiotics (APUA)
75 Kneeland Street, 2nd floor
Boston, Mass. 02111
617-636-0966

Animal Health Institute
1325 G Street, N.W.
Suite 700
Washington, D.C. 20005
202-637-2440

Centers for Disease Control and Prevention
1600 Clifton Road
Atlanta, Ga. 30333
404-639-3311

Food and Drug Administration
5600 Fishers Lane
Rockville, Md. 20857-0001
888-463-6332

The Soap and Detergent Association
1500 K Street, NW
Suite 300
Washington, D.C. 20005
202-347-2900

Union of Concerned Scientists
2 Brattle Square
Cambridge, Mass. 02238-9105
617-547-5552

World Health Organization
Avenue Appia 20
1211 Geneva 27
Switzerland

Further Reading

Books

Day, Nancy. *Killer Superbugs: The Story of Drug-Resistant Diseases*. Berkeley Heights, N.J.: Enslow Publishers, Inc., 2001.

Farrell, Jean. *Invisible Enemies: Stories of Infectious Disease*. New York: Farrar, Straus and Giroux, 1998.

Friedlander, Mark P., and Leonard T. Kurland. *Outbreak: Disease Detectives at Work*. Minneapolis, Minn.: Lerner Publications, 2000.

Latta, Sara L. *Food Poisoning and Foodborne Diseases*. Berkeley Heights, N.J.: Enslow Publishers, Inc., 1999.

Morgan, Sally. *Germ Killers: Fighting Disease*. Chicago: Heinemann Library, 2002.

Snedden, Robert. *Fighting Infectious Diseases*. Chicago: Heinemann Library, 2000.

Internet Addresses

American Society for Microbiology
MicrobeWorld
   <http://www.microbeworld.org/home.htm>

Centers for Disease Control and Prevention
Get Smart: Know When Antibiotics Work
   <http://www.cdc.gov/drugresistance/community/>

Food and Drug Administration
Antibiotic Resistance
   <http://www.fda.gov/oc/opacom/hottopics/anti_resist.html>

Index

A

Abbott Laboratories, 46
AIDS (acquired immune deficiency
    syndrome), 11, 28, 58–61
Alliance for the Prudent Use of
    Antibiotics, 41, 74
American Academy of Pediatrics, 37
amoxycillin, 30, 37, 73, 74
amphotericin β, 25
Animal Health Institute, 44,
    50, 57
animal use of antibiotics, 42–44,
    46–47, 49–52
anthrax, 46, 70, 71
antibacterial products, 52–56
antibiotics. *See also* names of
    individual antibiotics.
    development of resistance to,
        25–27
    discovery of, 21–24
    how they work, 24–25
    ineffective against viruses,
        25, 30
    misuse and overuse, 29–31,
        34–37
    production of, 29
    research and development (R&D)
        costs, 74, 90, 92
antimicrobials, 20, 23, 25, 27, 37, 39,
    56, 57
antiviral drugs, 27, 59
artemisinin-based combination
    therapies (ACTs), 70
avoparcin, 47, 50

B

bacterial cell division, 18–19
bacteriophages, 20, 83–85, 87
Bayer, 46, 50
BCG vaccine, 68, 89

Besser, Richard, 30–31, 35, 37, 94
Biophage Pharma, 85
bioterrorism, 46, 58, 70–72
botulism, 71
broad-spectrum antibiotics, 30, 32

C

Campylobacter jejuni, 44, 46
ceftiofur, 47
ceftriaxone, 47
Centers for Disease Control and
    Prevention (CDC), 30–31, 32, 35,
    37, 39, 41, 71, 72, 89, 94
cephalosporins, 25
Chain, Ernst, 22
chloroquine, 69
cholera, 16
ciprofloxacin (Cipro), 46, 72
Clostridium difficile, 32
Cocoanut Grove fire, 23
colds, 31, 61
conjugation, 20, 26
ConjuGon Inc., 82
Cornebacterium diphtheriae, 83
costs of drug-resistant diseases, 12–13,
    92–93
Cubicin, 79
Cubist Pharmaceuticals, 79

D

daptomycin, 79
de Freudenreich, Edouard, 21
d'Herelle, Felix, 83
Dial Corporation, 55
diarrhea, 17, 32, 46
diphtheria, 83
Direct Observed Treatment Short-
    course (DOTS), 66–67
DNA, 17–20
Dubus, René, 26

E

ear infections, 13, 36–37
economic impacts in developing
    countries, 65–66, 69–70, 90
efflux pumps, 27
Ehrlich, Paul, 21
Eliava, George, 83
Eliava Institute, 83–84, 85
emerging infectious diseases, 11–12
Enterococcus, 10, 27, 33, 47, 49, 50, 93
environmental concerns, 56–57
erythromycin, 6, 25, 26, 36
Escherichia coli (E. coli), 44, 85
Evergreen State College, 83, 85
Exponential Biotherapies, 85

F

Fischler, George, 55
Fleming, Alexander, 21–22, 26
Florey, Howard, 22, 23
fluoroquinolones, 44, 46, 89
Food and Drug Administration
    (FDA), 37, 41, 43, 46, 49, 50, 74,
    76, 78, 79, 82, 87
foodborne disease, 9, 49
foreign aid, 90–91
Foster Farms, 51
fungi, 16, 21, 52

G

Gertler, Alfred, 84, 87
Giardia lamblia, 17
gonorrhea, 9, 89
"good" bacteria, 16, 32, 82
Gram, Hans Christian, 18
gram-positive or gram-negative, 18
growth promoters, 43–44, 47, 49–52

H

Hancock, Brandon, 5–6
hand washing, 39, 52, 94
Hantavirus pulmonary syndrome, 11
Hata, Sahachiro, 21

HIV (human immunodeficiency
    virus), 11, 28, 58–61, 94
hospital-acquired infections, 9–10, 33,
    39–40
hospitals' infection control measures,
    39–40
hygiene hypothesis, 53, 55

I

intravenous immunogammaglobulin
    (IVIG), 80
Intralytix, 85
isoniazid, 64, 65

K

kanamycin, 26
Keep Antibiotics Working, 41
Klebsiella pneumoniae, 10
Koch, Robert, 16
Kutter, Elizabeth, 83, 84–85, 87

L

Lederle Laboratories, 43
Levy, Stuart B., 34, 40, 44, 53, 54, 74

M

macrolides, 89
macrophages, 62
malaria, 13, 17, 58, 68–70, 88
managed-care programs, 35
McDonald's, 51–52
meningitis, 10, 13, 23
methicillin, 6, 10, 26, 73
methicillin-resistant *Staphylococcus
    aureus* (MRSA), 6, 7–11, 39, 40
multi-drug-resistant tuberculosis
    (MDR-TB), 65, 67–68
mutations, 19, 26, 41, 59

N

Nabi Biopharmaceuticals, 80
nalidixic acid, 25
National Chicken Council, 57
National Tuberculosis Center, 61

neomycin, 26
nosocomial infections, 9–10, 33, 39–40

O

opportunistic infections, 60–61
over-the-counter (OTC) drugs, 31–32, 89

P

Pasteur, Louis, 16
penicillin, 6, 21–23, 25, 26, 30, 36, 73, 89
peptides, 79, 80, 82
Perdue Farms, 51
personal health habits, 94–95, 97
Pfizer Inc., 75
phage. *See* bacteriophage.
PhageTech, 85
"pirate" drugs, 60, 90
plague, 70–71
plasmids, 18, 20, 34, 46
Plasmodium, 17, 68
pneumonia, 10, 13, 20, 61, 64, 79–80
polymycins, 25
Powers, John, 37, 41, 74
prescriptions, 29–31, 34–37, 39, 40, 72
Prevnar, 79
prions, 17
prisons, 10–11, 64, 67, 93
probiotics, 82
Projan, Steven, 76, 78–79
protists, 16, 17
Pseudomonas, 10, 20, 21

Q

quarantine, 93–94
quinolones, 25

R

Rastafarianism, 93
Reichman, Lee, 61
research and development (R&D), 74, 90, 92

resistance genes, 25, 33–34
retrovirus, 58–59
Rhone-Poulen Rorer, 49
ribosomes, 18, 25
Rib-X Pharmaceuticals, 79
rifampin, 25, 26, 64–65
Rockefeller University, 85
Russia, 13, 67–68, 71

S

Salmonella, 33, 46–47
Salvarsan, 21
selective pressure, 6–7, 10, 13, 25–27, 29, 32, 39, 40, 53, 56
SIGA Technologies, 79
Silbergeld, Ellen K., 46
smallpox, 11, 71–72
Soap and Detergent Association, 54–55
StaphVAX, 80
Staphylococcus, 5–6, 7–9, 10–11, 21, 26, 40, 80, 82, 93
Streptococcus, 10, 13, 36, 40, 80, 89
streptomycin, 23, 26, 44, 64
sudden acute respiratory syndrome (SARS), 89
sulfadoxine-pyrimethamine, 69
sulfonamides, 23, 25, 26
Synercid, 49, 93

T

tetracycline, 25, 27, 47, 89
toxic shock syndrome, 80
travel, 88–89
Trichomas vaginalis, 17
triclocarban, 52
triclosan, 52–53, 55, 56
tuberculosis (TB), 11–12, 13, 16, 23, 58, 61–68, 80, 88, 90, 93, 94
tularemia, 24, 71
Twort, Edward, 83
Tygacil, 76, 78
Tyson Foods, 51

U

Union of Concerned Scientists, 41, 44
urinary tract infections (UTIs), 23, 33

V

vaccines, 11, 27, 60, 68, 71–72,
    79–80, 89
vancomycin, 6, 9, 27, 33, 39, 47, 49,
    74, 93
vancomycin-resistant *Enterococcus*
    (VRE), 33, 39, 40, 47, 49
van Leeuwenhoek, Antonie, 16
virginiamycin, 49
viruses, 11, 17, 20, 25, 27–28, 30,
    35–36, 58–61, 71, 83

W

Waksman, Selman, 23–24, 64
Walker, Polly, 46
wastewater, 16, 44, 56, 83, 85
World Health Organization (WHO),
    12, 13, 41, 65, 66, 67, 90
Wyeth Pharmaceuticals, 76, 78

Y

Yersinia pestis, 70–71

Z

Zithromax, 75
Zyvox, 93